The dragon is the most ancient and widespread of all monsters. Dragon legends are told in every culture and in every continent on Earth. Its breath condenses and forms rain in China. It slithers across the heavens in Mexico as Quetzalcoatl. In Scandinavian lore its coils encircled the whole earth. No other monster is so universal in its occurrence or so varied.

But the British Isles are the homeland of the dragon. Although a small country, it is seething with dragon legends. *Explore Dragons* puts British dragon stories into their international context and attempts to fathom out what really lurks behind these fanciful tales. Could dragons once have been real creatures? Are such creatures still alive?

Richard Freeman is a former zookeeper and has a degree in zoology. He is the zoological director of the Centre for Fortean Zoology in Exeter. A full-time cryptozoologist, he has searched for monsters and mystery animals in Indo-China, Sumatra, and Mongolia as well as in the UK.

The aim of Heart of Albion's 'Explore' series is to provide accessible introductions to folklore and mythology. Some books provide 'overviews' of quite broad topics, drawing together current academic research with popular beliefs. Other books in the series deal with more specific topics, but still with the aim of providing a wide-ranging introduction to the topic.

Series editor: Bob Trubshaw

Other titles in the 'Explore' series include:

Explore Folklore Bob Trubshaw

Explore Mythology Bob Trubshaw

Explore Green Men Mercia MacDermott

Explore Shamanism Alby Stone

Explore Fairy Traditions Jeremy Harte

Explore Phantom Black Dogs edited by Bob Trubshaw

Explore Hinduism Bansi Pandit

EXPLORE DRAGONS

Richard Freeman

Heart of Albion

EXPLORE DRAGONS

Richard Freeman

Cover illustration by Ian Brown

ISBN 1 872883 93 1

EAN 978 1872 883 939

Published by
Explore Books
an imprint of
Heart of Albion Press
2 Cross Hill Close, Wymeswold
Loughborough, LE12 6UJ

albion@indigogroup.co.uk

Visit our Web site: www.hoap.co.uk

Printed in England by Booksprint

For Lisa Dowley

Contents

List of illustrations

Following page: The book wyrm by Ian Brown.

Introduction

Strange as it may sound I am a monster hunter. It is what I do for a living: hunting monsters. I am a fully qualified zoologist and once was Head of Reptiles at a major British zoo. Why then, you might ask, did I give that all up to chase creatures that the majority of people do not even believe exist?

The answer is quite simple. The world is not the cosy, well-explored, safe place you might think it is. Vast areas of our planet are still unexplored and uninhabited. Every year new species of large animal are discovered – most recently, a type of primitive hog called a 'peccary' in South America. Moreover, hundreds of people all over the globe report encounters with strange creatures every year. Can they all be liars or victims of hoaxes?

There is even a science dedicated to the study of unknown creatures. It is called 'cryptozoology',—a word coined by Belgian zoologist Bernard Heuvelmans in the 1950s. Heuvelmans is regarded as the father of the science. I am one of only a handful of full-time professional cryptozoologists in the world. This is no hobby. It is my life's work.

I am also the zoological director of the Centre for Fortean Zoology, the world's only fulltime mystery animal research organization. The word 'Fortean' is derived from the American writer, researcher and philosopher Charles Hoy Fort (1874–1932). Fort noticed that mainstream science was acting more like a religion than anything else. Any data that fell outside of the known remit at the time was rejected without being properly examined. Fort called this outcast data 'the dammed'.

Monsters and mystery beasts are part of 'the dammed', despite turning up with alarming regularity. The kraken was a multi-armed monster from Scandinavian maritime lore until the 1870s when it began to wash up alive and kicking. Now we call it 'the giant squid'. The famous mountain gorilla was nothing but a hairy giant from native legend until 1904. Despite the wilful blindness of most mainstream scientists monsters still stalk the Earth in the twenty-first century.

In May of 2005 I led an expedition to the Gobi Desert in Mongolia. The purpose of the trip was, ostensibly, to search for a creature known as the Mongolia deathworm, a two-foot long, burrowing, sausage-shaped creature rumoured to be highly venomous. We interviewed many witnesses far flung in both distance and time whose descriptions tallied very well. Though we did not see the deathworm ourselves we concluded it existed and was probably an unknown species of sand boa or worm lizard, a reptile rather than a true worm.

As well as the deathworm we were told of other strange beasts that inhabited the trackless wastes of the Gobi. One was a species of large (two metre) horned snake, the other was a dragon, not a big snake or lizard but a literal dragon.

One man who worked programming computers for a mining company in the Mongolian capital Ulan Batar told a very strange story. His aunt related to him what she had seen shortly after the Second World War close to a remote village in the north of the country. One harsh winter they had found a huge, dead, elongated animal frozen in a nearby river. It was around 30 metres long and covered with scales. They called it a dragon. Only the upper half of it was visible above the ice. The winter was particularly hard and the villagers survived by eating the flesh of the dead creature. The remains were washed away by the spring thaws.

In the deep Gobi we heard several stories of dragons inhabiting wells. These were not just from the mouths of peasants and nomads. Just twelve months previously a qualified doctor from Ulan Batar had been visiting the remote town of Bulgan Sum.

Whilst drawing water from the well he saw what he described as a 'Chinese dragon', green in colour coiled at the bottom of the well.

What was it this educated man saw? He insisted it was a dragon. We in the West have been taught from childhood that the dragon is a fictional creature confined to storybooks and fairytales. This is not so in other parts of the world. Sightings of dragon-like creatures occur far more often around the globe than most people would ever imagine. I have also met dragon witnesses in Thailand and Sumatra but not all such encounters happen so far away from home.

The dragon is the most ancient and widespread of all monsters. It is the great grandfather of monsters, the '*über* monster' if you will. The dragon is found in every culture and in every continent on Earth. Its breath condenses and forms rain in China. It slithers across the heavens in Mexico as Quetzalcoatl. In Scandinavian lore its coils encircled the whole earth. No other monster is so universal in its occurrence or so varied.

But the homeland of the dragon is Great Britain. For such a small country it is positively seething with dragon legends. In this book I will look into British dragon stories and try to fathom out what lurks behind them. Could, at the core of these fanciful tales, lie a real creature?

Chapter 1
Types of British dragon

Ask any child to draw a dragon and they will probably produce a winged, scaly quadruped. An out-sized lizard with bat's pinions spitting fire. This is the dragon we are most familiar with. It is cast as the villain in numerous childhood stories. It was the wicked adversary of numerous heroes such as Beowulf and Saint George. It thrills us as Smaug in Tolkien's timeless classic *The Hobbit*.

However many more types of dragon are to be found in British folklore. As well as the winged fire-spitting monsters we can find limbless venom-spewing beasts, water-dwelling creatures, and tiny serpents so deadly that their mere gaze can strike a man dead. Let us take a closer look at the dragon fauna of the British Isles.

The true dragon

Also known as the heraldic dragon or firedrake this is the dragon *par excellence* – the most well-known of all dragon types and the most widespread and the most powerful. The true dragon is a gigantic reptilian beast with four legs. It sports two leather, bat-like wings and is covered with armoured scales. Its head is usually depicted with horns or a crest. It has a spined tail and savage teeth and claws. Its main weapon however is its breath. The true dragon's most famous attribute is the jets of flame spitting from its jaws.

This was the ultimate challenge for a folk hero or knight. The true dragon was almost impossible to kill. It had only one vulnerable spot on its whole body and this was usually well hidden. In many (though not all) legends these creatures protect a horde of treasure. They are also attributed magical powers such as invisibility and self-healing. Dragons such as these often laid waste to vast areas and put whole communities under siege.

The true dragon occurs more often than any other type in British legend.

The worm

Sometimes rendered 'wyrm' (from the Norse *orm* and the Germanic *vurm*) the worm runs a close second in its number of appearances in British legends. It is, in essence, a titanic snake. These limbless giants often grew from tiny innocuous looking serpents, a motif also found in the folklore of China and Scandinavia.

Worms did not breathe fire but spat venom or belched blasts of poisonous gas. A worm would often poison whole areas and cause crops to wither. As well as its deadly bite and breath, the worm crushed its prey in monstrous coils like an outsized python or anaconda.

Worms also had some odd attributes. They seemed fond of milk (an odd diet for a reptile) and would often suckle from cows. Some were placated by being given troughs of milk. They were also renowned for being able to rejoin severed sections of their bodies, making them exceedingly hard to kill.

The wyvern

The wyvern resembles the true dragon in many ways. It is a reptilian, winged monster that brings death and destruction. It fulfils the same role in legends as its relative – a guardian of treasure, and an obstacle to be defeated by a hero. The main difference between the two creatures is that the wyvern has only two legs, in contrast to the dragon's four legs. Many wyverns sport scorpion-like stings in their tails. They have bat's wings, and a snake-like head and neck. The legs are eagle-like, with curved talons. The head is often furnished with horns or a crest. Wyverns were generally smaller than true dragons. Most wyverns flew but some were earthbound and crawled despite having wings.

Wyverns were believed to carry diseases, spreading pestilence wherever they appeared. Plague outbreaks and illnesses of both humans and livestock were blamed on them. Some wyverns breathed fire in the fashion of true dragons. Others spewed forth a noxious poison gas.

The basilisk or cockatrice

Of all British dragons the basilisk is the smallest, most being only a few feet long at their maximum. It was believed that occasionally – in old age – a rooster could lay an egg. If such an uncommon egg

Call of the wyvern. Drawing by Ian Brown.

were to be incubated by a snake or toad, then a basilisk would hatch.

What the basilisk lacked in size it made up for in deadliness. Its death-dealing powers came not from fiery breath or tooth and claw but from its withering glare. Any creature that caught the eyes of the basilisk would fall dead. The one exception was the weasel. It was believed that God never created a bane without creating some cure for it (as with the stinging nettle and the dock leaf). The monster's own gaze was as lethal to itself as to any other creature. Hence, its own reflection would kill it stone dead! Equally – for some cryptic-reason – the sound of a cock crowing at dawn would also kill the basilisk.

The basilisk usually took the form of a small snake with a crest resembling a rooster's comb or a crown. In later stories they looked like a horned rooster with a snake's tail.

In this form it was referred to as a cockatrice.

The gwiber

The gwiber is a legless winged serpent. In appearance it is half-way between the wyvern and the worm. The word 'gwiber' is a corruption of 'viper'. Most of the British winged serpent stories come from Wales. In Wales gwibers actually outnumber the more familiar type of dragon that we see even today on the Welsh flag. Gwibers did not usually breathe fire but they had a highly venomous bite.

The Welsh had some strange folklore pertaining to the genesis of the gwiber. It was believed that serpents loved milk and would – given the chance – suckle from cows. Women's milk was favoured even more, but if an ordinary snake drank the milk of a woman it would grow into a gwiber. Nursing-women had to be careful not to let any of their milk fall to the floor where a snake might lap it up, or to fall asleep on the ground where a snake might reach their breasts.

Another strange quirk of Welsh gwiber tales is that they are never killed by a knight or any sort of nobleman. It is always a shepherd, farmhand or some other peasant-lad who puts paid to the gwiber by using his wits.

Odds and ends

Some British dragons do not fall into any particular category. One is the serpent of Handale in Yorkshire. This beast had a crested head and spat fire like a true dragon. It bore a sting like a wyvern. However it had no limbs and was in effect a giant snake.

The dragon or dragons of Wormingford and Bures on the Essex-Suffolk border resembled a true dragon but lacked the fire-breathing powers and huge wings of these monsters.

The cockatrice of Castle Gwys in Dyfed had a body covered with hundreds of eyes but unlike its kin this monster's gaze did not seem to kill. Conversely the dragon of Castle Carlton had only one huge eye.

Chapter Two
Gazetteer of British dragons

No other country on Earth packs so many dragons into so little space. Although tiny, the British Isles are teeming with dragons. In later chapters we will search for answers to why this should be. For now we will take a county-by-county whistle-stop tour looking at each and every one of the surviving dragon legends.

England

CHESHIRE

Moston

Sir Thomas Venables slew a water-dwelling dragon here to save a child. He managed to kill it by shooting an arrow through its eye. His reward was a grant of land that the fortunes of the Venables family were founded on. The family crest shows a dragon with a child in its jaws.

Runcorn

A dragon sporting tiger-like stripes along its scaly body once lived on the banks of the Mersey. It was coated in impenetrable scales and had eaten every single cow for miles around. A blacksmith called Robert Byrch had an idea. He put a cow's hide and horns over a metal framework and hid inside holding a sword.

The dragon saw what it thought was a cow and swooped down to grab the animal in its claws. The dragon lifted the *faux* cow and the farmer high into the air and was flying across the Mersey when the farmer stabbed his assailant in its one vulnerable spot, beneath the wing. Losing height rapidly the mortally wounded monster reached the far bank and expired.

The King knighted Robert as Sir Robert Bold and granted him as much land as the dragon's hide could contain. He cut the monster's hide into thin strips and encircled an area known to this day as Bold's Heath.

The cow's hide complete with the slashes made by the dragon's claws was displayed until the 1870's in Farnworth Church.

CORNWALL

Helston

Here a huge fire-breathing dragon was seen flying over the town. It clutched a ball of flames in its claws. The dragon dropped the flaming mass just outside the town where it cooled down and formed a huge rock that is still there.

Padstow

Padstow is famous for its hobby 'oss (more of which later) but it was also once inhabited by a dragon. Saint Petroc was said to have tamed it by placing a girdle about its neck. The dragon was then led down to the seashore and let loose. It swam away and never bothered anyone again.

CUMBRIA

Hayes Water

A dragon lived in a pond together with a giant char (fish). It caused little trouble but would stir up the water on occasion.

Renwick

A bat-winged cockatrice lived in an old church spire. In 1733 it objected to the church's demolition and flew out to attack the workers. All fled except John Tallantine who slew it with a stake made from hawthorn. For this deed he and his descendants were exempt from paying tithes

DERBYSHIRE

Drakelow

A dragon is mentioned in a document dating to 772 as being buried in a prehistoric burial mound. It is interesting to note that 'drake' is derived from *draco*, Old English for dragon and 'low' from *hlwa*, Old English for burial mound. Perhaps this indicates a dragon guarding a burial mound.

Winlatter Rock

Two linked stories are attached to this area close to Chesterfield. The first concerns a dragon, reckoned to be none other than the Devil himself. He came from the north burning and destroying all in his path. A priest challenged him by climbing to the top of Winlatter Rock and spreading his arms in the form of a cross. The dragon called up great winds and storms to lash the holy man but he stood so firm that his feet sunk into the rock. The dragon turned back and Chesterfield was saved. The priest's footprints were etched into the rock and pilgrims would visit them for years afterwards.

The story has a sequel. Years later the dragon returned and picked up where he had left of, spreading destruction. Three brothers took a massive iron bar to the blacksmith and asked him to forge a sword.

'You won't be able to lift it,' the smithy said. 'One can't but three can,' the brothers answered. Then they met a farmer while they were carrying the sword to Winlatter Rock. 'You'll never carry it to the top of the rock,' he said. 'One can't but three can,' the brothers answered.

On the rock they saw a shepherd and told him that they were carrying the sword to the summit. 'You'll never get it up there' said the shepherd. 'One can't but three can,' the brothers answered.

Once they were at the summit one lad put the sword into the priest's footprint. One ran to Chesterfield to call the men at arms. And one went to the church and climbed up the steeple to ring the bell when the dragon came into view.

The bells rang out as the dragon flew towards town spewing fire and surrounded by a maelstrom of winds. It threw a lightning bolt at the sword and the weapon was lit up like a torch. The men at arms converged on the rock and all held up their swords like a forest of crosses. The dragon turned and fled down the Blue John Mines and remains there to this day. As he fled his tail struck the spire of Chesterfield church and twisted it out of shape. The twisted spire is still visible.

DEVON

Challacombe

Fire-breathing, winged dragons were seen at night. They flew around snorting fire and would perch upon Bronze Age burial mounds. Perhaps they were supposed to be guarding the contents.

Exeter

An enormous winged dragon was said to fly nightly over the Exe Valley lighting up the sky with its flaming breath. It flew back and forth between Dolbury Hill and Cadbury Castle guarding two hordes of treasure. A local saying goes...

> 'If Cadbury Castle and Dolbury Hill delven were
> All England might plough with a golden share.'

In this case no hero was forthcoming to do battle with the dragon.

Manaton

A winged dragon made its lair in an old tin mine here. Its hissing was said to be audible for miles around. It was finally slain in the mine but history does not record by whom. The story was recorded by the late eighteenth century writer Richard Polwhele. Devonshire dragon stories all seem to be frustratingly vague.

Winkleigh

Two seventeenth century writers recorded a brace of dragons here but there are no more details. A scant story even by Devon standards!

DURHAM

Bishop Auckland

The story here is very like that at Sockburn. But the species here is the limbless worm. The great serpent inhabited an oak wood and gobbled up man and beast. It was slain by a champion from the well-known local family, the Pollards. A falchion was the weapon of choice here as well. When the Bishop of Durham entered the diocese he would be presented with the sword.

Pollard was given a grant of land. It was as much as he could ride around while the bishop was at dinner. Pollard sneakily rode around the bishop's castle. The bishop refused to give up his home so Pollard was given a far greater estate instead, much larger than he could have ever rode around in the time allotted.

Durham

In 1563 a huge serpent was exhibited (presumably stuffed) in Durham. It had supposedly killed 1000 people in Ethiopia. It was almost certainly a crocodile.

THE LAMBTON WORM

The Lambton Worm, as depicted by Herbert Cole for Ernest Rhys's book Fairy Gold *(1906). (Fortean Picture Library).*

Lambton

On of the best-known British dragon legends is that of the Lambton worm. The story goes that Sir John Lambton, the young heir to Lambton Castle, went fishing one Sunday morning instead of going to church. He caught a small, horrid, snake-like creature on his line. Disgusted he threw it down a well and forgot about it.

Sometime later he joined up in the Crusades and travelled to the Holy Land. While he was away the snaky creature in the well grew to massive proportions and emerged to wreak havoc on the surrounding land. It ate livestock, sucked the milk from cows, and ate people. It had its lair on an island in the middle of the River Wear.

Many tried to slay it but it could rejoin severed portions of its body and hence always emerged triumphant. The people began to pacify it with troughs of milk. Once the milk was watered down and the worm sensed the deceit it went on the rampage.

Word reached Sir John Lambton who realised that the worm was the very creature he had caught but now grown to mind-boggling proportions. He returned from the Crusade and sought advice. Sir John visited a witch, Elspat of the Glen, who told him how the worm might be beaten. But before she gave the information she made the knight swear an oath. He must kill the first living creature that he met after the battle or a curse would fall upon the Lambtons and nine generations of the family would meet with untimely deaths.

The witch said that he must weld spikes to his armour to prevent the worm constricting him. He must also fight it in the middle of the River Wear where the current was strongest. This would wash away the segments of the worm's body before they could rejoin.

Sir John followed the witch's advice and arranged for his father to release a hunting dog for him to kill after the fight. The worm was fought in the middle of the river and all went to plan. The coils were severed and washed away before they could rejoin.

When he reached the bank his father was so overjoyed that he forgot to release the dog and rushed down to greet his son. Sir John could not kill his father so the curse fell. Nine generations of Lambtons did not die in their beds.

Sockburn

Prior to the Norman Conquest Sir John Conyers slew a man-eating dragon of some type. Before he did battle he went, in full armour, to the church and offered up his only son to the Holy Ghost. Up until 1826 each newly-elected Bishop of Durham was presented with the sword Sir John used in the fight, the Conyers Falchion. The sword actually dates from the thirteenth century so it cannot be the original. It is probably a facsimile created as the older weapon rusted away over the ages.

Oddly, in recorded manuscripts and civil speeches the exact species of dragon cannot be decided upon. The creature is referred to as a dragon, a flying serpent, a worm, or a wyvern. Almost the whole draconic gamut!

ESSEX

Henham

Robert Winstantley of Saffron Walden wrote a pamphlet titled *A True Relation of a Monsterous Serpent seen at Henham on the Mount in Saffron Walden* published in 1699. The creature in question was a winged serpent (that would have been called a gwiber in Wales) that appeared in May of that year. It was around nine feet long and as thick as a man's leg. Its eyes were as large as sheep's eyes and it had several rows of sharp teeth. It was also furnished with small wings.

Despite having caused no trouble its demeanour was sufficiently alarming that a group of villagers armed with farm implements and stones chased it off.

Horndon

The dragon of Horndon was said to have been imported (presumably as a youngster) in the Middle Ages by Barbary merchants from whom it escaped. It set up home in the surrounding forest and grew to huge proportions.

It was eventually killed by Sir James Tyrell who managed to dazzle the dragon by wearing highly-polished armour.

Saffron Walden

The pamphlet that deals with the Henham winged serpent also relates the story of a basilisk that held siege to Saffron Walden centuries before. It was described as:

'... not about a foot in length, of colour between
black and yellow, having very red eyes, a sharp head
and a white spot hereon like a crown. It goeth not
winding like other serpents but upright on its breast. If
a man touch it though with a long pole it kills him:
and if it sees a man a far off it destroys him with its
looks. Furthermore it breaketh stones, blasteth all
plants with his breath, it burneth everything it goeth
over; no herb can grow near the place of his abode.'

The basilisk killed so many people that the town was becoming depopulated. Finally a wandering knight delivered them by covering his armour in crystal glass. On seeing its own reflection the monster died.

The Romanesque dragon's head inside Deerhurst church. Did this 'severed head' inspire the local legend? Photograph Bob Trubshaw

St Osyth

A broad sheet produced in 1704 refers to a dragon of 'marvellous bigness' being discovered here during the reign on Henry II. Nothing more is known about this creature.

GLOUCESTERSHIRE

Deerhurst

The Deerhurst dragon was covered in impenetrable scales and fed on livestock. It killed villagers with its deadly breath. It was finally slain by a local labourer, the exotically named John Smith.

John set out a trough of milk for the dragon who greedily drank the lot. After its meal it stretched out to sleep. Whilst sleeping the dragon ruffled up its scales in the manner of a bird fluffing its feathers. Seeing his chance John took up an axe and struck between the scales, hacking off the monster's head.

HAMPSHIRE

Bisterne

The Bisterne dragon dwelt on Burley Beacon, a hill in the New Forest. Two versions of this story exist. In one of the accounts the dragon is placated by being fed milk by the local villagers. They grow weary of paying this tribute and hire a knight, Sir Macdonie de Berkeley, to slay the monster. The knight takes a jug of milk to lure the dragon and a cabinet of mirrored glass to hide in. When the beast was busy slurping the milk he stepped out from his hiding place and slew it.

The second version is far more dramatic. The knight is called Sir Maurice de Berkeley. The dragon in this story was not to be fobbed off with milk. It gorged on livestock and human flesh. Sir Maurice fought it accompanied by two huge mastiffs. Prior to the battle he covered his armour in birdlime and ground glass. Both the dogs and the knight died along with the dragon.

Wherwell

A duck's egg was incubated by a toad in the cellar of Wherwell Priory. It grew into a cockatrice and set about withering all around it. A reward of four acres of land was offered to anyone who could kill the beast. Several champions came forward only to be slain by the deadly glare of the cockatrice.

Finally a priory servant named Green lowered a polished steel mirror into its cellar lair. Unlike most of its kin the Wherwell cockatrice's reflection was not instantaneously lethal to it. It took its own reflection for another, rival cockatrice and attacked it. Once it had exhausted itself fighting its own image Green leapt down and killed it with a spear.

Up until the 1930s older residents of Wherwell refused to eat duck's eggs!

HEREFORDSHIRE

Brinsop

St George is said to have killed a well-dwelling dragon in a field called Lower Stanks. A twelfth century stone carving in the church shows him spearing a worm type dragon.

*The twelfth century tympanum now inside Brinsop church.
Photograph Fortean Picture Library.*

Mordiford

The story of the Mordiford wyvern is one of the most detailed dragon legends in Britain as well as being the one with the most variations – no less than five.

A young girl called Maud was walking through woods when she found a baby wyvern, bright green and no bigger than a cucumber. She took it home to keep as a pet, feeding it on milk. It grew very fast and began to eat chickens, then sheep, before graduating onto cows. Finally as an adult it turned man-eater, though it remained friendly towards Maud. It made its lair on a ridge in Hauge Wood and always followed the same path, known to this day as Serpent Path, to the river.

Locals now took steps to end its reign of terror. This is where the stories diverge. In one variation the hero is a criminal under sentence of death. He is promised his life and freedom if he kills the wyvern. He is lucky enough to find it asleep in its den and kills it bringing the tongue back for proof.

17

Another version says the same hero hid in a cider barrel by the wyvern's drinking place, the confluence of the rivers Wye and Lugg. He shot it through the barrel's bunghole.

Another more exciting twist is that the barrel was covered with hooks and blades. The wyvern spotting the man inside coiled around the barrel but mortally wounded itself on the spikes.

In all of the first three of these variations the hero dies from the wyvern's breath.

Yet another ending has the wyvern gorging itself on a drowned ox then being surrounded and killed by villagers while it sleeps off its meal.

Finally one story says the hero was not a criminal but a member of a distinguished local family, the Garstons.

The story had such a hold over the locals that in 1875 the rector found two of his parishioners, a pair of old women, trying to drown some newts in the belief that they would grow into wyverns!

Wormelow Tump

Dragons are said to guard treasures in two prehistoric burial mounds, Wormelow Tump and Old Field Barrows.

HERTFORDSHIRE

Berkhamsted

St Paul, while visiting Britain was supposed to have banished forever all snakes, dragons and thunderstorms. He didn't do a very good job!

Brent Pelham

A mighty dragon made its lair under the roots of an ancient yew tree and wrought havoc in the surrounding countryside. Piers Shonks, Lord of the Manor of Pelham, fought it accompanied by three huge hounds. He finally triumphed by thrusting a long spear down its throat.

At the moment of victory the Devil appeared vowing vengeance on Shonks for destroying his beast. He swore that he would have Shonk's soul whether he was buried inside nor outside the church.

Shonks foiled the Devil by being buried in a cavity within the church wall and hence neither inside or outside of the church.

St Albans

This is the scene of one of Britain's oldest dragon legends. Abbot Ealdred of St Albans, who succeeded office in 1007, rebuilt his abbey using the ruins of Verulamium, a Roman city nearby. During the course of the demolitions he was said to have flattened the lair of the dragon of Wormenhert. There is no information on the dragon itself or what it was doing before the abbot destroyed its den.

LANCASHIRE

Unsworth

A manor house in this town, owned by the ancient family of Unsworth depicts Saint George and the dragon together with a unicorn, a lion, an eagle and a child. Legend has it that the table was carved with a dagger that slew a dragon. The man–eating beast was invulnerable to bullets on account of its scales. Thomas Unsworth loaded a dagger into his gun and shot between the monster's fangs and down its gullet.

LINCOLNSHIRE

Anwick

While ploughing a boggy field a farmer saw one of his horses sucked down into quicksand. Just as the horse vanished a huge dragon flew out of the bog. The next day a boulder in the shape of a dragon's head appeared in the field.

Stories began to circulate that treasure was beneath the boulder and many tried to raise it but none succeeded. The dragon was sometimes seen flying up from the bog but never seemed interested in attacking anyone. The boulder is still there to this day but has broken in two.

Castle Carlton

The Castle Carlton dragon was unique among British dragons in that it had only one huge eye, the size of a basin, in its forehead. It was slain by Sir Hugh Bardolfe who fought the creature during a thunderstorm. A flash of lightning dazzled the dragon long enough for Sir Hugh to strike its one vulnerable spot, a wart on one of its legs.

Walmsgate

A dragon is said to be buried under a long barrow here. The town's original name may have been Wormsgate.

NORFOLK

Ludham

A fire-breathing dragon struck fear into the hearts of the Ludham residents. Upon discovering its cave they tried blocking the entrance but the dragon merely tore away the rubble. Finally, one man found a boulder that was the exact shape of the cave entrance and blocked it up while the dragon was out.

On finding its cave blocked the dragon moved to the vaults under the ruins of the Abbey of St Benedict.

NORTHUMBERLAND

Bamburgh

The Laidly (Northumbrian dialect for 'loathsome') worm was once a beautiful princess who lived in Bamburgh castle. Her stepmother was a witch who, out of jealousy, cast a spell changing her into a huge worm. The worm's breath caused vegetation to shrivel and it demanded the milk of seven cows every day.

Depending on which of the two versions you hear, the hero is either Margaret's brother Child Wynd or a man named Kemp Owen. Not knowing that the worm is in fact the princess he sets out to slay it. When he confronts the worm it tells him to put down his sword and kiss it three times upon its ugly head.

> 'O quit your sword, unbend your bow,
> And give me kisses three
> For though I am a poisonous worm
> No harm I'll do to thee.'

Amazingly the hero co-operates and the worm transforms back into Margaret.

The curse rebounds and the witch is turned into a toad that hops off down a well. Some say the toad reappears every seven years and can be changed back into human shape by a hero kissing her after unsheathing Child Wynd's sword and blowing three times on his horn.

Longwitton

A green dragon lurked by three holy wells in the grounds of Longwitton Hall. It had the power to make itself invisible and heal any wounds. It did not terrorise the area like others of its kind but kept people away from the wells.

Sir Guy of Warwick was asked to free the wells and rode out to fight the dragon. It became visible when it attacked him. The knight was no match for the dragon's flaming breath and teeth and claws. He barely escaped alive.

After recuperating he and his horse returned for a second bout with the dragon. This time he noticed that on the few occasions his sword penetrated the monster's scales almost instantly its wounds healed. He also noticed that it kept the tip of its tail in one of the wells. Once again Sir Guy was almost killed. But he realised that the dragon was drawing healing power from the well.

After licking his wounds again he challenged the beast again but this time with a plan. Feigning defeat he staggered away from the well. The dragon followed and its tail drew clear of the well. Sir Guy positioned his horse between the dragon and the well and took up the battle again. Finally he was able to deliver a fatal wound to the monster while it was away from the well's healing power.

OXFORDSHIRE

Dragon Hill

Close to the more famous White Horse Hill this small flat-topped hill is one of the places St George is supposed to have slain the dragon. The dragon's blood burned the soil at the top of the hill so that no grass will grow there.

In fact St George was a Syrian con man and never set foot in Britain, let alone fought a dragon! More of this shady character later.

SOMERSET

Aller

The dragon of Aller was a terrifying beast. It spat both fire and venom and flew on vast leathery wings. Its lair was a hillside cave just outside of Aller and, as Western dragons are wont to do, laid waste to the land.

The dragon was finally slain by John of Aller. There are two versions of the story; in one John is a knight, in the other a lowly peasant. He covered himself in pitch and wore a mask to protect himself from the dragon's breath. After a terrible battle he was able to thrust a long spear down the dragon's throat and killed it. In one version of the story John is burnt to death by the dragon's breath, in another John survives and finds a brood of hatchlings in the dragon's cave. The cave is subsequently blocked up.

21

St Carantoc subduing the Somerset dragon. Drawing by Ian Brown.

Carhampton

In Arthurian legend Saint Carantoc visited this part of Somerset while looking for his altar. He met with King Arthur who was worried about a dragon terrorising the county. Arthur knew the whereabouts of the Saint's altar and said he would reveal it if Carantoc rid him of the dragon.

Early sixteenth century bench end in Crowcombe church depicting the slaying of the local dragon. Photograph Fortean Picture Library.

The saint tamed the dragon by putting his stole around its neck and leading it to Dunster castle. An angry mob wanted to attack the now placid beast but Carantoc would not let them. He released the dragon after telling it to harm no one ever again.

Castle Neroche

A treasure-guarding dragon once lived here but that is all that remains of this legend.

Churchstanton

A dragon once resided in the place were Stapley Farm now stands. After causing the usual havoc it was slain by an anonymous knight. The lashing of the dragon's tail is said to have carved out a hollow in a field known as Wormstall.

Crowcombe

In Shervage Wood near Crowcombe lived a worm thicker about the middle than an oak tree. It fed on local livestock then expanded its diet to humans. It ate two gypsies and a shepherd. The locals became too afraid to enter the wood to pick bilberries for making pies.

One old woman asked a woodcutter from the village of Stogumber, a few miles from Crowcombe, to pick some berries for her. The kind-hearted man agreed. After picking an abundance of the fruit he sat down to eat bread and cheese and drink cider. The man thought he was sitting on a dead tree but when it began to writhe about he realised to his horror that the 'log' was in fact the worm. He hoisted his axe and cut the monster in two.

Lucky for the woodcutter the worm was disorientated. One half slithered off towards Minehead and the other towards Taunton. So rather than recombining the segments both perished.

Kingston St Mary

A savage fire-breathing dragon terrorised this area until a champion came forth to tackle it. He rolled a boulder up a hill opposite the dragon's lair and shouted out to it. As the monster emerged with its jaws agape he rolled the boulder down into its mouth choking it before it could roast him with a jet of flame. (Because of changes to county boundaries Kingston St Mary is now part of Dorset but was previously in Somerset.)

Kilve

A dragon called Blue Ben resided here and was supposedly the steed of the devil. He fell from a causeway of rocks and drowned in the mud. His skull (actually a fossil ichthyosaur) was uncovered and is on display in the local museum.

Norton Fitzwarren

Here the Roman general Ostorius was said to have killed hundreds of ancient Britons. Over the centuries a dragon grew from the corruption of the rotting bodies (this spontaneous growth of creatures from rotting matter was commonplace belief in medieval times). It took up residence in an Iron Age hill fort and preyed on the populace until Fulk Fitzwarine, a thirteenth century knight, slew it. Despite his brave deed Fulk fell foul of King John and was exiled. He continued his adventures abroad when he saved the Duke of Iberia's daughter from a dragon near Carthage.

Trull

A dragon was supposedly slain on Castleman's Hill near Trull but no details are known. The local church has a stained glass window showing saints George, Michael and Margaret killing dragons.

Wells

Bishop Jocelyn supposedly drove out a dragon that had been terrorising locals around seven holy springs. The cathedral was built next to the springs.

Wiveliscombe

In 1827 when the church here was being rebuilt the Devil manifested riding a green dragon and began hurling rocks at the church. Saint Andrew then materialised and drove them off with a cross.

SUFFOLK

Bures / Wormingford

Confusion and controversy surround this legend on the Suffolk / Essex border. Both the town of Bures and the village of Wormingford lay claim to the story as their own.

In a nineteenth century translation of a document from 1405 the story is told of a fearful dragon, that had a hide impenetrable to arrows and disappeared into marsh after having caused 'much hurt'.

Wormingford begs to differ saying that the creature resided there and was finally killed by Sir George de la Haye.

Little Cornard

Two dragons did battle here. A spotted red dragon from Ballingdon Hill on the Essex side of the River Stour came down to fight a black dragon from Kedington Hill on the Suffolk side. After a long battle the red dragon won. Both dragons survived the fight and returned to their respective lairs.

A contemporary document recording these events is held in Canterbury Cathedral.

SURREY

West Clandon

A dragon lived in a lane here, making villagers afraid to walk along it. The monster was finally slain by a soldier and his dog. The soldier had been condemned for desertion but promised a pardon if he could kill the dragon. He managed to thrust his bayonet into the beast's venerable spot when his trusty hound distracted it.

SUSSEX

Bignor

A huge worm wrapped itself around Bignor Hill and left the imprint of its coils on the hill.

Cissbury

A prehistoric earthwork on the South Downs is supposed to contain a huge treasure horde. A tunnel reputedly runs from the earthwork to Offington Hall, two miles away. In the 1860s the owner of the hall offered half the treasure to anyone who could clear out the tunnel and find the horde. Several people tried but were driven back by huge snakes that sprang hissing at them with open mouths.

Fittleworth

As recently as 1867 a worm was supposed to reside here and rush out hissing at anyone who passed by its lair.

Lyminster

Here we have another dragon legend of which three different versions exist. The dragon was known as the Knucker and inhabited a supposedly bottomless pool known as the Knucker Hole.

In the first version the dragon is terrorising the area and has eaten all the maidens leaving only the King of Sussex's daughter. The King offers his daughter's hand in marriage to anyone who can deliver her from the dragon's jaws. A wandering knight took up the challenge and slew the beast.

Others say it was a local lad named Jim Puttock who feeds the dragon an indigestible pudding and then kills it while it is indisposed with a bout of bellyache! He gets some of its poisonous blood on his hand and, after wiping his mouth after a celebratory pint of beer, he dies.

The third variation Jim bakes a poisoned pie so huge it needs a horse and cart to transport it to the Knucker Hole. The dragon eats the pie – along with the cart and the horse – and subsequently dies.

Knucker is believed to derive from *nikyr*, Old Norse for water monster.

St Leonard's Forest

This was once vast forest of the Weald. St Leonard himself was supposed to have fought a dragon in its depths. Where the Saint's blood fell patches of Lily of the Valley sprung up.

In 1614 another type of dragon appeared in the forest, a limbless worm some nine feet long that killed both man and beast with poison and for a while became infamous in the area.

WORCESTERSHIRE

Wolverley

A document dating to 1582 refers to a place called Drakelow as being inhabited by a dragon. Nothing however is known of the dragon or indeed the place.

Once again we see Drake, a corruption of the Old English *draco*, and *low* derived from *hlaw* or burial mound. *Ergo* a dragon guarding a burial mound.

YORKSHIRE

Bilsdale

A dragon was said to reside in a prehistoric burial mound guarding treasure.

Cawthorne

A flying serpent dwelt in Serpent's Well and would fly from there to Cawthorne Park.

Filey

The dragon of Filey was defeated not by a knight but a timid, hen-pecked little tailor named Billy Biter. One misty morning he fell into the dragon's lair. As the dragon was about to eat him he offered it some parkin, a sweet, sticky Yorkshire pudding. The monster liked it so much it demanded more.

When Billy told his nagging over-bearing wife she insisted that she cooked the parkin and took it to the dragon. The dragon so disliked Billy's wife that it ate her as well as the parkin. Her cooking was so bad that the pudding stuck the dragon's jaws together.

He went to the sea to wash it out but was overcome by the icy waves. His bones turned to stone and became Filey Brigg, a promontory of rock that stretches a mile out to sea. In the 1930s there was a report of a sea dragon seen on Filey Brigg by a coastguard.

Handale

The woods near Handale Priory were inhabited by a crested, fire-spitting worm with a sting in its tail. It made a habit of eating maidens until it was slain by a youth named Scraw. Scraw found an earl's daughter in the worm's cave and rescued her. His reward was her hand in marriage and vast estates. The wood was known as Scraw's Wood from then on.

Kellington

Although quite a way from Loschy Hill and Slingsby, the story of the Kellington worm runs much the same as the legends associated with them (see below). Here the worm dwells in a marshy forest and is fought by a shepherd called Ormroyd (*orm* being Norse for dragon).He was aided by his dog who ended up with the monster's poisonous blood on his muzzle. After the worm was killed the shepherd bent down to stroke his dog which then licked his face, transferring some of the poison. Both man and dog died. Perhaps would-be dragon slayers should avoid bringing their dogs along!

Sexhow

A winged fire-breathing dragon terrorised the area and took up residence on a hill. It demanded the milk of nine cows every day. As well as breathing fire it belched poison gas, killing anyone who ventured too close. It was finally killed after a long battle with a wandering knight who then went on his way without demanding a reward or revealing his name.

The dragon was skinned and its hide taken to Stokesley church where it hung for many years. It vanished many years ago.

Slingsby

Sir William Wyvill, whose family was known to have lived in Slingsby in the fourteenth century, did battle with a worm. He covered his armour in razor blades before the fight. The monster could rejoin severed sections of its body so the knight brought with him his trusty hound who snatched up the pieces of the monster's coils and ran off with them to preventing them rejoining.

After the worm was vanquished the knight bent down to pet his dog and it licked his face. Both man and hound died from the monster's venomous blood.

The worm's lair, according to a seventeenth century document, was a great round hole three yards wide and half a mile from town. The worm was thought to be over a mile long.

Stonegrave

Loschy Hill is a few scant miles from Slingsby and the legend here is so like the latter that they may share one root legend. The fight with the worm, assisted by the dog and the death by worm blood is exactly the same. Here, however the knight is Sir Peter Loschy and the dog ran to the village of Nunnington one mile distant to deposit the bits of worm.

Wantley

Here lived a fire spewing, winged dragon that devoured not only humans and animals but ate up trees. The knight who did battle with the beast was almost as formidable. More of More Hall was a huge man who reputedly killed a horse with his bare hands after it had angered him. He then ate it.

The night before the battle More had a black haired maiden of sixteen anoint him. His armour was covered, like so many other dragon slayers, with spikes each six inches long. The fight raged between man and beast for two days and a night. Neither opponent could get a palpable hit on the other. The dragon finally grabbed More, intending to throw him high into the air like a rag doll. More managed to kick a spiked boot into the dragon's only vulnerable spot, its backside!

Well

The dragon of Well was slain by a knight named Latimer who was a local landowner. A dragon is featured in the Latimer coat of arms.

Jersey

La Hogue Bie

Seigneur de Hambye, Lord of the Manor, slew a fearful dragon after a long and awful combat. While lying wounded and exhausted after the fight his squire crept up and murdered him. The squire returned to the village claiming to have killed the dragon himself after it had killed his master. He married his master's widow and acquired his lands. His chicanery was later found out after he suffered nightmares and spoke in his sleep.

Scotland

ANGUS

Strathmartin

Here a dragon guarded a well. It ate nine maidens one by one who came to draw water. It was finally slain by a man named Martin who was the lover of one of the girls.

ARGYLLSHIRE

Ben Vair

The hero of this story was a sea captain, Charles the Skipper. He came up with a trap to rid the area of a dragon that was the bane of all. He anchored his ship a little way offshore and built a bridge from the vessel to the beach. It was made of barrels lashed together and studded with metal spikes.

Then he began to roast some meat on his ship. The smell wafted to the dragon's lair and it came swooping down to the beach. As it began to crawl across the bridge of barrels the spikes pierced its hide and one struck the vulnerable spot. The massive beast expired on the bridge long before it got to the ship.

KIRKCUDBRIGHTSHIRE

Dalry

The worm here was white in colour and this legend may have inspired Bram Stoker's novel *Lair of the White Worm*. It wound itself around Mote Hill and got up to the usual tricks.

A local blacksmith made a suit of armour covered with retractable spikes. He allowed the worm to swallow him and then wriggled so violently in its gut that the monster's intestines were shredded.

Solway Firth

A sea-dwelling worm devoured fish stocks that the local people depended on. Not satisfied with seafood it crawled ashore to eat farm animals and humans. People from the villages along the shore built a huge palisade of sharpened stakes and erected it at low tide. When the worm came in with high tide it became impaled on the spikes.

Its roaring and death throws lasted for three days. Sea birds ate its carcass.

Orkneys

For sheer size the Stoor Worm rivals the Norse Jormungand or Midgaurd Serpent. It was so vast that when it yawned the Earth shook and great waves spewed over the land. Its breath was a vast cloud of poison that withered crops on the land. Its monster tongue was so huge it could sweep whole villages into its mouth.

In desperation villagers consulted a wizard who told them that the only way to keep the Stoor Worm at bay was to feed it seven virgins each week. This was duly done until the time came for the king to sacrifice his own daughter. He offered her in marriage to anyone who could slay the worm.

The young hero, Assipattle, now puts in an appearance. The youngest of seven sons of a well-to-do farmer he had been branded a good-for-nothing dreamer all his life. He stole his father's fastest horse and rode away from the farm. He also stole an iron pot of burning peat from an old woman. Finally he stole a boat and went out to sea.

He got close enough to the Stoor Worm that when it yawned he was drawn into its mouth. He travelled for miles down the vast gullet. Eventually he comes came to the worm's liver which glowed with an eerie phosphorescence. He cut open the liver and thrust the red hot pot inside. The liver ignited and began to burn fiercely.

In its death throws the worm vomited up its stomach's contents, including Assipattle. Its thrashing caused tidal waves, volcanic eruptions and earthquakes. After it died its teeth formed the Orkney Islands and the Shetlands. Its body became Iceland and its tongue the Baltic Sea. The still-burning liver became Iceland's volcanoes.

Somehow Assipattle survived all this and married the princess.

ROSS AND CROMARTY

Loch Maree

Until the middle of the eighteenth century bulls were sacrificed on 25th August (St Maerlrubha's Day) to dragons that dwelt in the lake. These may have been kin to the creatures still reported in other Scottish lochs to this day. We shall examine them in a later chapter.

ROXBURGHSHIRE

Linton

The Linton worm was perhaps the laziest British dragon. It lived in a cave on Linton Hill and instead of actively hunting its prey it would suck passing animals and people into its waiting mouth.

After eating, it would crawl out of the lair and coil around the hill leaving deep impressions. Local peasants offered a reward to whosoever could slay the worm. The knight who took up the challenge was the Laird of Linton who was from Somerville.

He attached a lump of peat to a wheel that he then fitted to the end of his lance. He dipped the peat in boiling pitch, brimstone and resin. He set light to the concoction and charged at the worm, ramming it down the beast's throat.

He was also rewarded by being given the post of Royal Falconer to the King of Scotland.

SUTHERLAND

Conc na Cnoimh

The story here is very like that of the Linton Worm. The hero was a farmer named Hector Gunn. He used a spear seven ells (585 inches or nearly 16 metres) long. He fitted a lump of peat to the end and dipped it in boiling pitch. The fumes were so bad that they stopped the worm from attacking him. He rammed it between the worm's jaws and in its death throws its squeezing coils were wrapped about the hill. Gunn was rewarded by the king with lands and money. The king was said to be William the Lion who reigned in the twelfth century.

Conc na Cnoimh means 'Hill of the Worm'.

Wales

ANGLESEY

Penmynydd

In this detailed story a rich nobleman invites a soothsayer to the celebration feast after his son's birth. The sage foretells the boy will die of a gwiber's bite. The boy is sent away to England for safekeeping and his father offers a reward to whoever can slay the last gwiber in the area.

A clever lad digs a pit on the path where the gwiber usually slithers. At the bottom he places a highly polished brass mirror. He covers the pit with sticks and grass then waits. The gwiber falls into the pit and sees its own reflection. Thinking it a rival it attacks the mirror until exhausted. Then the boy leaps into the pit and hacks off its head.

Years later the nobleman's son now a spoilt teenager returns and is shown the gwiber's skull. He contemptuously kicks it and one of its long-dead fangs slices through his boot. The fang retains traces of venom and, as prophesied the boy dies.

CARDIFF

A worm was supposed to live at the bottom of a whirlpool in the River Taff. It was said to drown people and suck down their bodies to eat.

CARMARTHENSHIRE

Newcastle Emlyn

A flame-spewing wyvern laired in a ruined castle. It was covered in impenetrable scales. A soldier waded into the river with a large piece of red cloth. The wyvern reacted to the cloth like a bull (or a male robin) and swooped down to attack it. This allowed the soldier to shoot it in its one vulnerable spot. Like the dragon of Wantley, the vital spot was its rear end!

Trellech a'r Betws

A gwiber is supposed to guard a prehistoric burial mound in the area.

CONWAY

Betws y Coed

A monster known as the Wybrant gwiber terrorised the neighbourhood. An outlaw from Hiraethog tried to kill it but it bit him, tore out his throat and flung him into the river for good measure!

Cynwch Lake

A wyvern dwelt in this lake beneath the slopes of Moel Offrum. It emerged to poison the countryside and devour whatever it could catch. The Wizard of Ganllwyd employed a group of archers to kill it but it always avoided them.

One day a shepherd boy named Meredydd found it sleeping on the hill. He ran two miles to Cymmer Abbey and borrowed a magic axe. He struck the wyvern's head off while it slept.

Llyn y Gadair

In the eighteenth century a group of men were swimming across this small lake close to Snowdon. One of them was grabbed and devoured by a worm.

Nant Gwynant

After the Roman legions left, Vortigern became the first British king. He decided to build a stronghold on the Iron Age hill fort of Dinas Emrys. Each time work began it was destroyed by earthquake-like disturbances. His wizards said that in order to stop these events the ground should be sprinkled with the blood of a virgin's son. A boy was found whose mother had apparently been magically impregnated by a spirit. He was about to be sacrificed when he went into a trance and announced that beneath the hill was a lake. In the lake dwelt a red dragon and a white dragon who perpetually fought.

Vortigern's men dug down and found a lake. When the lake was drained they found a pair of dragons. The two great reptiles fought until at last the white dragon gave way and fled. Seeing this as an omen that his forces would defeat the invading Saxons, Vortigern adopted the red dragon as his emblem.

The boy was none other than a young Merlin.

PEMBROKESHIRE

Castle Gwys

In one of the strangest British dragon legends the beast here was a cockatrice whose body was covered in eyes. For some unexplained reason the estates of Wiston were up for grabs to whoever could look on the freakish thing without it seeing them.

One resourceful chap hid inside a barrel and rolled into the cockatrice's lair. He shouted out 'Ha, bold cockatrice! I can see you but you cannot see me!'

He was granted the estates. What happened to the multi-eye monster is anyone's guess.

POWYS

Llandeilo Graban

A dragon roosted in the tower of Llandeilo Graban church until a local ploughboy worked out a way of destroying it. He carved a dummy dragon out of oak and had the blacksmith cover it with steel hooks and spikes. It was then painted red and erected on the tower while the dragon was away hunting.

Upon returning the dragon saw what it thought was a rival and savagely attacked it. The real dragon coiled about its facsimile and tried to squeeze the life from it. The genuine article became fatally wounded and the dragon and its lure came crashing down from the tower in ruin.

Llanrhaeadr-ym-Mochnant

A gwiber brought a reign of terror to the area until the surviving locals studded a huge megalith with spikes and hooks and swathed it in red cloth. The red colour enraged the gwiber who attacked becoming fatally entwined on the hooks. The megalith is known as Red Pillar of the Viper.

VALE OF GLAMORGAN

Penllyn

Brilliantly coloured flying serpents were said to inhabit the woods of Penllyn as recently as the mid-nineteenth century. People who were old men and women at the beginning of the twentieth century recalled them well from their youth. They were prone to raid chicken coops and as a result were hunted into extinction.

Penmark

Another colony of the winged serpents resided here. One old woman said her grandfather had killed one after a fierce fight. She recalled seeing the skin preserved at his house when she was a girl. To the horror of cryptozoologists it was thrown away upon his death.

Chapter Three
Who were the dragon slayers?

Saints

St George

There can be few heroes as famous as St George, or few as widely represented in art. From an early age we all recognise the image of a knight in shining armour, astride a white charger, bearing a red cross on his shield. He battles a flame-spewing monster to save a princess tethered out as a sacrifice. He represents purity, bravery, and nobility and is, of course, the patron saint of England. All of this pomp makes it a bigger shock to find out just what the real, historical St George was like.

The man who was to become St George was born in the third century in a fuller's shop in the city of Epiphania (now Hamath) in Syria. Little is known of his early life but as an adult he used servile flattery to climb the social ladder and reach a lucrative spot supplying the army with bacon.

He apparently amassed quite a large amount of money by dishonest and unscrupulous business practices. His chicanery was eventually uncovered and he had to fled the country.

He converted to a heretical sect, Arianism, that denied the divinity of Christ. He was so zealous in his adopted religion that the Roman Emperor Constantinus sent him to Alexandria to become an archbishop.

The real George was as cruel and greedy as any legendary dragon. He pillaged pagan temples and taxed both pagans and Christians beyond endurance. The people rose up and ousted him but the army of Constantinus swiftly reinstated him. However when Emperor Julianus came to power Alexandria reverted to paganism and George plus two of his most ardent followers were thrown into prison.

The trio remained incarcerated for twenty-four days until an angry mob smashed down the prison doors, beat them to death, carried

The valiant St George. Drawing by Ian Brown.

their bodies triumphantly through the streets and flung them into the sea. Death at the hands of the pagans in AD 303 made this obnoxious man a martyr.

When the Arians final re-entered the mainstream church they brought the man they had canonised with them. By the sixth century St George was established as a saint in the Catholic Church.

During the Crusades St George was said to have resurrected to fight alongside the Christians. He was said to have fought for Godfrey of Bouillion at the battle of Antioch and appeared to Richard the Lion Heart as a portent of victory.

Such unlikely shenanigans assured immortality for the Syrian pork swindler. The legend of the dragon was tacked on for good measure in the twelfth century. He became England's patron saint in 1284.

The dragon legend is heavily based on the Greek myth of Perseus and Andromeda. The sea monster Cetus is replaced with a swamp-dwelling dragon. The story runs thus:

A terrible dragon had ravaged all the country round a city of Libya, called Selena, making its lair in a marshy swamp. Its breath caused pestilence whenever it approached the town, so the people gave the monster two sheep every day to satisfy its hunger but, when the sheep failed, a human victim was necessary and lots were drawn to determine the victim. On one occasion the lot fell to the king's little daughter. The king offered all his wealth to purchase a substitute, but the people had pledged themselves that no substitutes should be allowed and so the maiden, dressed as a bride, was led to the marsh. There St George chanced to ride by and asked the maiden what she did, but she bade him leave her lest he also might perish. The good knight stayed, however, and, when the dragon appeared, St George, making the sign of the cross, bravely attacked and transfixed it with his lance. Then, asking the maiden for her girdle (an incident in the story which may possibly have something to do with St George's selection as patron of the Order of the Garter), he bound it round the neck of the monster, and thereupon the princess was able to lead it like a lamb. They then returned to the city, where St George bade the people have no fear but only be baptised, after which he cut off the dragon's head and the townsfolk were all converted.

In England, the Order of the Knights of St George was founded at Windsor Castle, and St George became the patron saint of England replacing the less glamorous Edward the Confessor. The Knights of St George have the garter as their emblem. This dates from a party on St George's Day (23rd April) in 1348. The host, Edward III, intervened when he found that the guests were giggling at Joan,

Duchess of Salisbury, whose blue ribbon garter had dropped off. He picked it up, tied it round his own knee and cried '*Honi soit qui mal y pense*' which, roughly translated, implies shame on anyone who thought ill of the garter-dropping incident, a phrase so eternally resonant that it now adorns many coins, courtrooms and family crests.

Edward III instantly abandoned his plans to form a new Round Table, and instigated instead the Order of the Garter. The blue ribbon became its badge of honour, first awarded one year later on St George's Day. The Order still exists, and Knight of the Garter is among the highest honours doled out by the monarch.

Joan's blue garter is explained by the fact that blue was said to be the saint's colour, and it remains customary to wear something blue on St George's Day. This justifies the wearing of bluebells today, as opposed to roses that are not in bloom on St George's Day, 23rd April.

As well as England he is patron saint of Greece, Germany, Italy, Malta, farmers and horsemen.

All in all this is not bad going for an underhanded bacon thief. One cannot help but wonder what he would have done if he really had met a dragon!

St Petroc

Our knowledge of St Petroc comes from two *Lives of Petroc* written in the Middle Ages and discovered in comparatively recent times in a library in Paris. A translation of the text of *The Vita Petroci,* written in the twelfth century, was published in 1930 by Canon G.H. Doble, under the title *St Petroc, Abbot and Confessor.*

Petroc was a Welsh nobleman who was educated in an Irish monastery, the major seats of learning in those days. He spurned his noble birthright and set out with a small band of followers, by sea, to spread the Gospel. The winds and tides brought him to the Padstow estuary.

With the help of the local inhabitants he began to build at the top of the creek (the sea level coming further in than at present) first a church and gradually other buildings, enlarging the establishment into a Celtic monastery complete with a school, infirmary, library, farm and cells for the monks.

Explore Dragons

Around this time a dragon was living near Padstow. Saint Petroc reputedly tamed it by placing a girdle about its neck. The dragon was then led down to the seashore and let loose where it swam away and never bothered anyone again.

Having established the monastery and church here, Petroc traveled widely, founding other churches, first in Little Petherick and Bodmin and then in many parts of Britain, Wales and Brittany.

The Celtic King Constantine ruled this area at that time and was said to have been converted to Christianity by St Petroc, when the saint rescued the deer that the king was hunting.

When old and sick Petroc was making his way home to Padstow, but died a few miles away at Treravel and his body was brought home by his companions. The year was 594.

His bones were stolen in the twelfth century and taken by a priest to the abbey of Meen in France. Such holy relics were a valuable asset to any church in those days. A priest was dispatched to ask for them back and he managed to persuade the abbey authorities to return the precious relics and searched for a suitable receptacle to contain them.

He purchased a painted ivory casket for the remains, which are at present held in St Petroc's Church, Bodmin.

He is patron saint of Cornwall.

St Carantoc

Less is known about this saint. He was a Celtic saint and is also referred to as Caranog, Carantus, Cranog and Carantacus. He was the son of Corun, ruler of south Wales. Like St Petroc he turned his back on the good life for a more holy existence and travelled the coastline of Britain. A number of churches are dedicated to him.

It is said he travelled to Ireland to assist an elderly St Patrick and he also founded several churches in France.

In Arthurian legend Saint Carantoc visited Carhampton in Somerset while looking for his altar. He met with King Arthur who was worried about a dragon terrorising the county. Arthur knew the whereabouts of the Saint's altar and said he would reveal it if Carantoc rid him of the dragon. The saint tamed the dragon by putting his stole around its neck and leading it to Dunster castle. An angry mob wanted to attack the now placid beast but Carantoc would not let them. He released the dragon after telling it to harm no one ever again.

Carantoc is patron saint of Somerset.

St Leonard

Yet another highborn man, this time of Frankish nobility, St Leonard gave it all up to become a hermit. He was born around 485. He once had success in persuading the pagan King Clovis I to release some prisoners and therefore people began to pray to him for the safe return of prisoners of war. Like St George he became much venerated by the Crusaders.

Apparently his prayers were believed to have aided the King's victors so he converted to Christianity.

There is no evidence he ever visited Britain, though there is a chapel dedicated to him in St Leonard's Forest, Sussex. The legend of him fighting the dragon there may have been a christianisation of an earlier story. There is no tradition of him fighting dragons anywhere outside of Britain.

His patronage includes horses, prisoners, blacksmiths, coal miners, coopers, coppersmiths and grocers.

St Andrew

Originally a Jew, no Hebrew name is recorded for Andrew. He was born at Bethsaida a city east of the River Jordan on the Lake of Galilee. He preached in Asia Minor along the Black Sea as far east as the River Volga.

He was crucified in Greece on a *crux decussata*, an 'X'-shaped cross more commonly known as the St Andrew's cross. According to tradition his relics were removed from Patras to Constantinople, and thence to St Andrews in Scotland in the middle of the eighth century.

His dragon-slaying exploits are quite recent and restricted to Wiveliscombe in Somerset where in 1827, when the church here was being rebuilt, the Devil manifested riding a green dragon and began hurling rocks at the church. Saint Andrew then materialised and drove them off with a cross.

He is the patron saint of Scotland, Russia, fishmongers, fishermen, singers and unmarried women.

St Paul

Born Saul at Tarsus, Cilicia (modern Turkey) in AD 3 he originally hated Christians and persecuted them. He supposedly took part in the stoning of St Stephen. On his way to Damascus to arrest another group of Christians he was knocked to the ground during a scuffle and apparently had a vision. After this he was converted to Christianity. He travelled to Arabia to preach and study, then travelled in southern Europe. He was beheaded in Rome in AD 65 after sufficiently annoying Jews and pagans.

Though there are no accounts of him fighting dragons on his missions his name is evoked against snakebite.

He is the patron saint of Poland, saddle makers, rope makers and newspaper editors.

Knights

Some knights in British dragon legends are anonymous heroes whose names are lost to history. But some of the named knights were real people with known histories.

Fulk Fitzwarine who fought the Norton Fitzwarren dragon was a real man. He had the misfortune to quarrel with King John and was then considered an outlaw. He moved abroad and then his travels took on a legendary quality. A long poem was written about them in French during the reign of Edward I. Branches of the Fitzwarine family are still extant and their family crest bears a dragon.

Sir John Lambton was a member of the Knights of St John in Rhodes, a group of Christian warriors whose chief job was foiling Barbary pirates and making reprisals on land against Islamic forces. Sir John was active with them in the mid-1400s. About a century earlier the Order's Grand Master had been Deodat de Gozon who had supposedly slain a dragon at Malpasso in Rhodes (centuries later the fossil skull of a hippo was believed to be the dragon's head). Some think that Sir John brought this story home and the dragon-slaying legend was incorporated into the family history with John as the hero.

The main problem with this is that the Rhodes dragon was a fire-breathing winged quadruped whereas the Lambton worm was a giant, limbless snake-like beast. The Lambton legend seems too detailed to be derived from the earlier story. As well as this the Lambton family were venerated long before the time of the worm legend so they would gain little by its creation. Regardless, Sir John was a real, historic figure.

Many British dragon stories are 'charter legends' used to explain how a certain family got its title or land. Sir Piers Shonks in the Brent Pelham story seems to have been a real man. His name was Peter Shank and he lived in the area in the fourteenth century. His family held property in the region including land and a manor house called Shonks. This is where the confusion about his name may have arisen. Peter was also granted another manor house in Barkway by Richard FitzAlan, the Earl of Arundel.

With the Bisterne dragon there is a deed dating from the time of Edward IV that conferred knighthood on Sir Maurice de Berkeley and gave him permission to wear the dragon as his badge.

Commoners

In a British dragon legend the hero is more likely than not to be a commoner. Twenty-six of the ninety or so dragon legends have a working man or group of working men doing battle with the monster. Knights make up twenty-four of the ninety. There are also five saints, an abbot and a bishop. Sometimes a whole community pools together to rid themselves of a monster such as the sea worm of Solway Firth, the gwiber of Llanrhaeadr ym Mochnant, one version of the Mordiford wyvern story, and the dragon of Bures. Sometimes the dragon is not slain at all.

Working class heroes include ploughboys, woodsmen, a sea captain, shepherds, a soldier, blacksmiths and even a tailor (or rather his dragon of a wife!). Sometimes the hero, who usually has a suitably dull name such as Jim or John wins the hand of a rich landowner's daughter in marriage. Sometimes he uncovers a great treasure. More usually he is just content to rid his people of a scourge. There are no heroines in British dragon lore, though the parkin made by Billy Biter's shrewish wife does for the dragon of Filey. Doing battle with dragons seems to be a male preserve.

One British dragon story has both a lowly convicted criminal and a nobleman vying for the status of hero. The wyvern of Mordiford was, in most of the many versions, killed by a criminal. In one variant it was a nobleman of the Garston family. A painting of the wyvern and an inscription once decorated the exterior wall of the local church. A Mr Broome, a historian from the area, described the inscription in 1670.

This is the true Effigy of that strange
Prodigious monster which our woods did range.
In Eastwood it by Garston's hand was slain
A true which old mythologists maintain.

In 1848 J. Dacres Devlin complied a booklet on the legend and
found that no one recalled the Garstons and that they all said it had
been a criminal who slew the wyvern. There had been, in the
seventeenth and eighteenth centuries, a family living in Mordiford
called Garston who had a wyvern in their crest. They had made
many donations to the parish. It is probable that the hero of the
original story was a member of the Garston family but after their line
had died out in the area the people came up with a working class
hero to replace him.

Tricks and tactics

Doing battle with a dragon is no easy task. Of all legendary beasts
they are unquestionably the most formidable, being covered in
diamond-hard scales, spewing fire and poison, and armed with
teeth, claws and a lashing tail. Some have the ability to self-heal or
become invisible. Dragon fighting was no picnic.

Some legends like those of Moston, Sexhow and Well contain no
details of the actual battle. These may have just been lost in time.
Where the battle is described it is usually an arduous affair often
leading to the death of the hero. Many British dragons are said to
have killed numerous would-be heroes before meeting their end.
Many also take down their killers with them.

The dragon's poisonous blood is sometimes to blame. Jim Puttock
envenoms himself by wiping his mouth. After slaying the Knucker
with a combination of poisoned pudding and a farm scythe he
celebrates with a pint of beer. Unfortunately he has some of the
Knucker's lethal blood on the back of his hand.

Sir Peter Loschy fell foul of worm's blood when his faithful dog
licked his face. The hound had been hauling away segments of the
Loschy Hill worm to prevent them rejoining after his master had
hacked them off. The blood proved fatal to both the knight and his
dog. Sir William Wyvill at Slingsby and the shepherd Ormroyd suffer
exactly the same fate with their dogs.

Sometimes the flaming breath of the dragon burns the hero to death.
John of Aller died this way when he thrust his spear down the
dragon of Aller's maw. Sir Maurice de Berkeley and his dogs died at

the fangs, claws and flaming exaltations of the Bisterne dragon. In three of the five versions of the Mordiford wyvern story the criminal hero dies at his moment of victory because of the beast's poison gas breath.

Sometimes a hero will find the vulnerable spot on a dragon, such as under the wing with the dragon of Runcorn. A long spear or lance thrust between the jaws is often used, as at Aller, Linton and Conc na Cnoimh. This makes perfect sense as the dragon's body is coated in a mail of scales. The one monster that proved exceedingly easy to slay was the Crowcombe worm as its segments crawled away from each other rather than rejoining as in other stories.

Getting the dragon to use its own great strength against itself is a good idea. All forms of dragon seem to be able to wind about their prey and squeeze the life out of it like a python. A good number of British dragon slayers have used this to their advantage. Sir John Lambton fastened spikes to his armour and Sir Peter Loschy used razor blades. The effect was the same, the worm only succeeded in wounding itself as it wound about the knight.

The nameless criminal who fought the Mordiford wyvern hides inside a barrel covered in spikes in one of the five variations of the story. The wyvern is mortally injured as it coils about the barrel trying to crush it.

More of More Hall who fought the dragon of Wantley was unable to pierce the dragon's hide with his spiked suit of armour so resorted to kicking it in the arse! The blacksmith who fought the white worm of Dalry went one better. He made the spikes on his suit retractable and allowed the worm to swallow him. He then sprang the spikes and slew the worm from within.

It has been suggested that the spiked armour idea was inspired by people watching battles between hedgehogs and adders. Surprisingly hedgehogs are fierce little carnivores. Not satisfied with slugs and worms they eat frogs, ground-nesting birds and small snakes. The adder will often mortally wound itself on the hedgehog's spines while trying to bite it. The spiky mammal curls up and sits tight for a while and then finds its foe moribund and a tasty meal awaiting.

Better than actually engaging the dragon in battle is to trick or bait it in some way thus avoiding combat. Spikes are used in these traps again. Charles the Skipper builds a spiked bridge of barrels and cooks some meat to trap the Ben Vair dragon. The sea worm of

Solway Firth is trapped on a huge palisade of stakes erected by fishermen.

Welsh dragons are enraged by the colour red. When backed up by the old favourite of spikes and hooks this is a very effective anti-dragon ploy. At Llanrhaeadr ym Mochnant a standing stone was fitted with spikes and swathed in red cloth to destroy a gwiber. In Llandeilo Graban a dragon was baited with a dummy rival painted red, furnished with spikes and hooks, and placed on top of the church tower where it roosted. A red cloth floated on a river was used to bait a wyvern to fly low enough for a hiding soldier to shoot its vulnerable spot (backside again!) at Newcastle Emlyn.

The use of mirrors or reflective surfaces are a recurring motif. Mirrored armour reflected the Saffron Walden basilisk's own deadly gaze back against itself. A polished metal mirror set at the bottom of a pit trap so enraged the gwiber of Penmynydd that it exhausted its strength and venom fighting its own reflection, allowing the hero an easy kill. The same trick was used on the cockatrice of Wherwell when a steel mirror was lowered into its lair.

On two occasions dragons are done to death by puddings. The Knucker of Lyminster is fed a giant poisoned pie and the dragon of Filey ate parkin so sticky that its jaws were glued shut and it fell into the sea while trying to wash it off.

Chapter Four
Clues and relics

Dragons do not just leave stories behind them. Sometimes they leave more tangible clues. Across Britain there are dragon relics like footprints in time. Hardly a town in the country does not have a dragon carving of some kind. But these relics are much more than church carvings. They include dragon-slaying weapons, physical marks on the landscape and, at one time, possibly biological remains.

Dragon skins

The Holy Grail for cryptozoologists would be a dragon scale, or piece of dragon hide. Such items were allegedly on display in various places in Britain.

A section of the hide of the Lambton worm was once held in Lambton Castle. It was said to resemble cow's hide. It was discarded when Lambton Castle was demolished in the eighteenth century.

The whole skin of the Sexhow dragon was hung at Stokesley church over the pew but has now long gone. F.W. Holliday enquired after it in the 1960s but the vicar had no idea what had happened to it. One theory is that the skin was actually a long cloth costume worn by villagers in some forgotten festival or mumming play. Then again it could have been the skin of a real animal.

The wings and skin of one of the small flying serpents said once to infest the area, was preserved on a farmhouse in Penmark. The farmer had killed the serpent after it attacked him. Tragically the remains were thrown away after his death in the nineteenth century.

We can only hope that sometime, somewhere in the world someone will be lucky enough to find some biological evidence of this greatest of zoological mysteries.

Dragon-slaying weapons

Some of the weapons supposedly used to slay dragons are still in existence and can be viewed by the public. The long spear that John of Aller thrust down a dragon's gullet in Somerset is held by a church. Strangely it is not the church in the village of Aller but at the church in Low Ham, a neighbouring village.

In Durham cathedral library resides the Conyers Falchion, a broadsword supposedly used by Sir John Conyers to slay the Sockburn Worm. It is decorated with dragons, lions and eagles from the Conyers coat of arms and dates from the thirteenth century. Up until 1826 the falchion was used in ceremony to greet each new Bishop of Durham. As the new Bishop crossed the River Tees he was greeted by the Lord of Sockburn Manor on the Croft Bridge and presented with the sword. The Lord then said:

> 'My lord Bishop. I here present you with the falchion wherewith the champion Conyers slew the worm, dragon or fiery flying serpent, which destroyed man, woman, and child; in memory whereof the King then reigning gave him the Manor of Sockburn to hold by this tenure, that upon the first entrance of every Bishop into the county this falchion should be presented.'

The ritual dates from the time of Bishop Hugh Pudsey during the rein of Richard I. It is mentioned in connection with the Death of Sir John in 1396. It was last performed in April 1826 when Dr Van Mildert, the last Prince-Bishop of Durham entered the diocese.

A manuscript kept in the British Museum runs thus.

> 'Sir John Conyers, knight, slew the monstrous and poisonous vermine, wyvern, asp, or werme, which had overthrown and devoured many people in fight; for that the scent of the poison was so strong that no person might abyde it. And by the providence of the Almighty God, the said John Conyers, knight, overthrew the said monster and slew it. But before he made this enterprise, having but one sonne, he went to the church of Sockbourn in compleat armour and offered up his only sonne to the Holy Ghost. The place where this great serpent lay was Greystone, and this John lyeth buried in Sockbourne Church in compleat armour of the time before the conquest.'

If the manuscript is correct then the fight took place before 1066 and the falchion is far too young to have been the actual weapon used.

St Michael subduing the dragon. Drawing by Ian Brown.

At Pollard's Dene, the land held by the Pollard family at Bishop Auckland, a similar ceremony took place. The land was granted to them after a heroic member of the family slew a huge worm that haunted an oak wood. On entering his diocese for the first time the Bishop of Durham would be presented with the Pollard falchion and the speech:

Avebury font. Photograph by Bob Trubshaw.

'My lord, I do humbly present your lordship with this
falchion at your first coming here, wherewith, as
tradition goeth, Pollard slew of old a great and
venomous serpent, which did much harm to man and
beast.'

The earliest record of this ceremony is from 1399.

The axe that John Smith used to kill the Deerhurst dragon was
supposedly retained by his family up until the eighteenth century.
No one knows what became of it after that.

The sword belonging to the knight who slew the Saffron Walden
basilisk was once kept in the local church. This was not used to kill
the creature, its death being affected by mirrored armour.
Parliamentarian soldiers destroyed the sword.

Carvings and images

To list every carving of dragons in Britain would take a thick tome
in itself. It would be pointless to detail every one. Therefore let us
look at a few of the most interesting examples.

Many church carvings such as the one at St Mary's in Knook,
Wiltshire shows a dragon guarding the Tree of Life. This is derived
from the Norse Yggdrassil or World Ash. This was essentially the

universe represented as a tree. Its roots are buried in hell and in its branches is Asguard, realm of the gods. The dragon Nidhorrg constantly gnaws at the ash, ripping great holes in its trunk. Three maidens called the Norns repair the dragon's damage.

This Nordic symbol was adopted by Christianity in the same way as many pagan festivals were. The Tree of Life encircled by a dragon occurs quite frequently in British churches. Other examples include the church at Burgh by Sands, Cumbria; Emley in Yorkshire; Wordwell in Norfolk, Thurleigh in Bedfordshire; Stratton in Gloucestershire; and Lullington in Somerset.

Unsurprisingly dragon slayings are a common theme in church carvings. The polar opposite of absorbing other religions these could be seen as Christianity driving other, older faiths out. St Michael is a favourite dragon-slayer. He is often shown as an angel armed with a shield and sword. A fine example is the north transept of Southwell Minster, Nottinghamshire. Christ himself is often shown trampling serpents or driving a cross down the gullets of dragons.

St George also does the rounds. The finest example is probably the one at Brinsop where he is depicted on a charger thrusting a lance into the mouth of a worm rather than a true dragon (see page 17). Wonderfully the tables are turned in the parish church in Tring, Hertfordshire. Here a mediaeval corbel shows the dragon killing St George – hurrah!

Sometimes a lowly bishop will do in place of a saint or a divine personage. The twelfth century font at Avebury Church shows a bishop and dragon in battle. The bishop is striking the dragon with his crosier while the dragon sinks its teeth into his foot.

Sometimes the carvings are directly linked to a local legend. For example the Sockburn dragon is associated with a large, weathered stone in the Conyers chapel, part of the ruined church of All Saints. On the stone is Sir John Conyers in chain mail with a sheathed sword. At his feet a lion and a dragon are fighting. The carving dates from the early fourteenth century.

At Deerhurst the church has no less than six depictions of the local dragon. One is outside the church and five more are inside (see page 15).

The Bisterne dragon is depicted in a sculpture over the door of Bisterne Park while the gallant dogs who died fighting him are commemorated in statues guarding the terraces of the gardens.

The ruins of Lambton Castle still hold a statue of Sir John Lambton in spiked armour slaying the worm. At one time there was a large stone trough from which the worm allegedly drunk its tribute of cow's milk.

The statue of a knight battling a dragon on foot that decorates Sheffield City Hall is said to represent More of More Hall fighting the dragon of Wantley.

Sometimes tombs are identified as belonging to dragon-slaying heroes. In the 1840s a stone coffin with an inscription so faded it was unreadable was discovered in the ruins of Handale priory. It contained an Elizabethan sword. Tradition had it that it was the grave and weapon of the dragon-slayer Scraw.

In the churchyard at Kellington there is a carved stone that looks like the lid of an ancient stone coffin. On it are carved a cross, a dog and a man. There are other marks suggesting age-worn illustrations that have faded away. It is supposedly the lid to the tomb of Ormroyd the shepherd who killed the Kellington worm with the aid of the dog. Some say the worm was depicted as well but has been worn away.

At Lyminster is another time-gnawed slab reputed to belong to the Knucker's slayer. It once stood near the main entrance to the church but has been moved inside it to stop it being further weathered. It shows a cross on a background of ribbing. This was interpreted as a sword and the dragon's ribs.

An elaborately carved monument, said to be the tomb of Piers Shonks, is set in a deep recess in the north wall of the nave at Brent Pelham church. Its marble cover shows an angel transporting a soul to heaven and a cross being thrust into a dragon's jaws. Its style seems to be thirteenth century.

Brass effigies of the basilisk of Saffron Walden were kept in the church along with the sword belonging to the knight who slew it. Both were destroyed by Roundheads during the Civil War.

At Mordiford a painting of the wyvern used to grace the west wall of the church. It was repainted a number of times and seemed to change with the whim of the artist.

John Aubrey who visited Mordiford in 1670 describes it as having six wings and two legs. The multiple wings may be meant to depict motion, the flapping of one pair of wings giving the illusion of many. Later it was repainted with four wings and two legs then finally with two wings and four legs. The painting was destroyed during church renovations in 1812.

A weather vane in the shape of the Wherwell cockatrice was made for the steeple of St Peter and the Holy Cross. It shows a monster with a bird's head, wings and talons with a coiling serpent's tail ending in an arrow shape. The weather vane is now in Andover Museum.

The steeple of the church of St Mary le Bow in Cheapside, London is graced with a fine dragon weather vane. The church was designed by Sir Christopher Wren after the mediaeval church that once stood there was burnt down in the Great Fire of London in 1666. The vane was built by coppersmith Robert Bird in 1679. He was paid the handsome sum of thirty-eight pounds for it, a small fortune in those days.

An even older dragon vane, dating from the sixteenth century can be seen at Newark Park, Ozleworth, Gloucestershire. This is possibly the oldest of its kind in the UK.

A dragon weather vane dating from the 1740s sits atop the chapel of Sir William Turner's Hospital near Redcar.

Unsurprisingly a dragon looks down upon the University College of Wales in Cardiff and another makes its home on the Washington Hotel in Llandudno.

In Haddenham, Buckinghamshire there is a veritable dragon track. Close to a lane called Dragon Trail there is a Green Dragon pub, close to this is Dragon Cottage complete with a dragon weather vane.

Speaking of pubs many British alehouses sport dragons on their signs. The Green Dragon is by far the most popular draconian name for a pub, though the Red Dragon is a popular name in Wales. Some pubs formerly called the Green Dragon changed their name to the George and Dragon in honour of George III.

Thomas Heywood in his 1608 book *The Rape of Lucrece* wrote a song on London pubs and their supposed clientele. He says prostitutes go to the Cockatrice. As far as I know no pub in London has that wonderful name today. There is however a pub called the Essex Serpent in Covent Garden. It is named after the Henham flying serpent that terrorised the county in 1669.

Ben Jonson in his comic work of 1601, *Every Man and his Humour* wrote, like Heywood, of London pubs and their patrons:

> 'The Saddlers will dine at the Saddle
> The Painters will go to the Green Dragon,
> The Dutchmen will go to the Froe,
> Where each man will drink his Flaggon.'

Dragon wells

A large number of British dragons are associated with wells. They may drink from them, dwell in them or guard them. It has been suggested that the well represents man's dominion over nature and his moulding of the natural world to his will. The dragon represents wildness and chaos that has to be tamed by man. Often the waters of the well are said to have curative powers. Another, perhaps better idea is that the dragon was or is a real creature with an affinity to water. This is an idea that we will be examining in detail in a later chapter.

Sir John Lambton threw an ugly worm-like creature he caught in the River Wear into a well where it lived for many years growing into the Lambton worm. The well still exists; it stands at the foot of Worm Hill, Penshaw. The worm supposedly left the marks of its coils upon the hill. The well was restored in 1974 and may be visited.

In the legend of the Dragon of Wantley the hero More of More Hall creeps down a well to ambush the dragon as he drinks. The event is recorded in a ballad:

> It is not strength that always wins,
> For wit doth strength excel;
> Which made our cunning champion
> Creep down into a well;
> Where he did think, this dragon would drink,
> And so he did in truth:
> And as he stoop'd low, he rose up and cry'd 'boh!'
> And hit him in the mouth.
> 'Oh' quoth the dragon, 'pox take thee, come out,
> Thou's disturb'st me in my drink.'

The well is still in existence but is in a poor state of repair. It is next to a natural spring.

Are dragons real creatures with an affinity for water?
Drawing by Ian Brown.

Mumming plays and civic processions

Dragons have been represented in plays and events all over the
British Isles for centuries. Their genesis was in the mediaeval mystery
plays. These consisted of troupes of travelling performers who

The Norwich 'Snap' dragon recreated by Nigel Pennick.

re-enacted stories from the Old and New Testaments. They carried with them costumes and props. The mouth of Hell was represented by a huge movable dragon's head. This emitted fire and smoke. Actors would pretend to be sinners devoured by the infernal beast. The serpent of Eden was also represented in a prop that must have resembled the Chinese dragons used to this day in processions in the Orient.

As the cult of that rascal St George grew in the late Middle Ages, his feast day, April 23rd became as important as Christmas and the celebrations grew accordingly. In Norwich the St George's Guild was formed in 1389. A re-enactment of George's apocryphal battle with the dragon began in 1408. The dragon was known as Snap and became a regular fixture of Norwich until 1843. In the original procession St George rescues a maiden identified as St Margaret from the dragon.

Snap consisted of a central, barrel-shaped cloth-covered framework in which his operator stood. A long cloth-covered neck protruded from the front terminating in a head with movable jaws. The jaws were operated by pulling a string. A metal plate in the mouth made a sharp snapping sound, hence his title. A tail counterbalanced the head at the rear. Two wings were set in the central frame. A cloth skirt hung down hiding the actor's legs. Two reptilian legs were painted on to the skirt making Snap a wyvern rather than a true dragon.

Initially a scary foe to the saint, Snap quickly became a more loveable figure. He would rush at the audience snapping his jaws to the delight of children. Snap survived the disbanding of the Guild of St George and the moving of the festivities from April 23rd to Midsummer. He also outlasted the two saints who were dropped from the shindig by dour Protestants in 1547.

Even without his old foe Snap was quite an eyeful. The parade began with six 'whifflers' who parted the crowds. Each carried a feather-decked rapier. They entertained the masses by juggling and catching the swords. They were followed by 'Dick Fools' in red and yellow canvas coats decorated with serpents and each carrying a dragon-headed stave with ribbon tongues and bells in their ears. Finally Snap himself arrived. Of course the costume was repaired and rebuilt over the years.

Snap's days finally became numbered by the Municipal Reforms Act of 1835 which banned such pageants, because they were considered to lead to drunkenness and disorder. Snap made irregular appearances up until 1850 and then was given to the Norwich Museum. This particular incarnation of Snap was constructed in 1795. Snap was brought out of retirement in 1988 when a new costume was created and he once again graced the streets of Norwich in the Lord Mayor's Parade.

Snap spawned kin at other locations. In Costessey, north-west of Norwich, another Snap stayed in the Whitsun pageant where he would follow dignitaries around five pubs throughout the day and end up at Costessey Hall in the evening. Another dragon paraded the streets of Little Walsingham, also in Norfolk.

A third Snap had his stomping ground in Pockthorp. Sometimes he would snatch a child's hat and only return it for a penny. This led to the rhyme:

> Snap, Snap
> Snatch a boy's cap.
> Give him a penny
> He'll give it you back.

Further afield a dragon made of canvass and wood was paraded in Newcastle upon Tyne in the fifteenth century, and a dragon and giant were paraded on Midsummer's Eve in Burford, Oxfordshire.

A major procession used to run through Leicester organised by the town's prestigious St George's Guild. The expense of four shillings for 'dryssynge the dragon' appears in the town's accounts for 1536–41. The custom was banned in 1546 (surviving records describe the sale of the 'the horse that George rode on' for 12d) but resumed for a few years before being lost between 1553–60.

Chester, Stratford upon Avon, and Lostwithiel in Cornwall also sported dragons on St George's Day.

These civic dragons were not limited to dry land. At the coronation of Henry VII a barge in the shape of a red dragon spewing flame was drawn along the Thames.

Henry VIII did not take so kindly to such frivolities. The Reformation attacked the idea of the divinity of saints. Henry VIII decreed that they could only be seen as 'fine human beings' and in 1538 halted the St George's Day procession through Canterbury. The statue of the saint was removed and destroyed. Up and down the country similar festivities were halted. Dragons and 'obby 'osses often suffered the same fate as St George.

In some areas festivities carried on in a somewhat watered-down form. A parade and service of the Knights of the Garter took place to display the country's principal chivalric order. It incensed the young Edward VI who complained, 'What saint is St George that we do here honour him?' The Marquis of Winchester replied 'St George mounted on his charger, out with his sword and ran through the dragon with his spear.' The young king sneered 'And pray you my lords, what did he do with his sword awhile?'

The parade was dropped in 1552 but returned triumphantly in 1555 under the Catholic Mary Tudor. Mary's husband Philip led the Knights of the Garter in their parade that included a dragon, a mock king (perhaps an effigy of Edward VI) and St Christopher. Other St George's Day parades returned countrywide and continued until the Protestant Reformation of Elizabeth. Once again statues were destroyed but Snap of Norwich survived until 1645, when any kind of saint's day celebrations were stamped on.

But you cannot keep a good dragon down. Snap was stalking the streets again in 1660 along with a new dragon in Chester who was attended by six naked boys!

Mummers plays often feature St George pitted against his old fiery foe alongside other characters as diverse as hobby-horses (or 'osses), green men, Morris dancers and even Father Christmas in later years. One troupe of mummers who performed at Revesby Hall, Lincolnshire in October 1779 said:

> We are come over the mire and moss,
> We dance an hobby-horse,
> A dragon you will see,
> And a wild worm for to flee.
> Still we are all brave jovial boys,
> And take delight in Christmas toys.

The performances have little to do with the original legends and it is unknown as to why and whence many of the seemingly spurious characters emerged. George will usually be killed by the dragon in the first bout but brought back to life by a doctor with a miraculous pill. He then triumphs in the second round. George is often shown fighting giants and Moorish knights as well. Different mumming troupes had differing plays.

St George boasts in the Salisbury version:

I slew the fiery dragon and brought him to his slaughter.
And by this deed I won for me the King of Egypt's daughter.

The Yatley mummers used King George himself as a character and his boast was just as great:

In comes I, King George, a man of courage bold,
With this broadsword and spear I won ten crowns gold.
It was me who fought that fiery dragon, and drove him to be slaughtered,
And by that means I won the King of Egypt's daughter.

When St George makes his entrance in the Burford mummer's play he shouts:

Here am I, St George
From Britain I did spring,
And I will fight the fiery Dragon
My wonders to begin.
I'll clip his wings,
He shall not fly;
I'll cut him down,
Or else I die.

The dragon answers:

Who is he that seeks the Dragon's blood?
And speaks so angry and so loud?
That English dog, will he before me stand?
I'll cut him down with my courageous hand.
With my long teeth and scurvy jaws
Of such I break up half a score.
Then stay my stomach till I have more.

Happily many of these traditions have survived and are still being performed today.

Hobby horses feature in many British pageants. The most famous are the 'Osses who caper about Padstow's streets on May Day. Hobby horses generally consist of a hoop with a tarpaulin or cloth draped over it to hide the operator's body. A weird, very unhorse-like mask is worn by the bearer. The mask usually has clacking jaws after the fashion of Snap. Some have suggested that 'obby 'osses were originally dragons and that they represented some vestige of an ancient pagan ritual. Exciting as that sounds it has now largely been debunked. Most of them date from the eighteenth century. Indeed the earliest reference to the Padstow ritual uncovered by E.C. Cawte and Roy Judge dated only to 1803. Even then the author of the account felt that it was not a Cornish tradition.

Some folk dances may have older pedigrees than the mumming plays. Robert Hunt, a Cornish folklorist, records a serpent dance that took place as recently as the nineteenth century in Roche, Cornwall as part of the Midsummer celebrations. A long line of dancers would wind into a meadow. The dancer at the 'head' end would lead the others in ever decreasing circles, round and round, forming serpent coils. Then the head would double back on itself and retrace the coils. All the time young men with leafy branches held like standards would direct the dancers. Its origin seems lost in the mists of time, but may well date from fairly recently. This may sound disappointing but we must remember folklore and tradition are evolving constantly. For example, the Walking of the Black Dog in Devon, where a huge effigy of one of the traditional phantom hounds is paraded for four miles down country lanes to Black Dog village. The festival was begun in the 1990s.

The descendants of Snap, the Norwich dragon, can be seen in every dragon float or dragon costume in every carnival the length and breath of the land. Snap has even become multicultural, hybridising with the beautiful Chinese dragons that so wonderfully enliven our streets during Chinese New Year. From his sinister beginnings as a symbol of evil and darkness he and his children now bring joy and wonder to audiences all across our land.

Chapter Five
Dragons around the world

The primary focus of this book is the British Isles but international dragon lore is so rich and fascinating that it would be remiss not to give the reader a taste of it. As mentioned before no country or culture on the planet has been untouched by the dragon. Around the globe it comes in many guises from death-dealing daemon to life-giving god and just about everything in between. A detailed examination of every country's dragon legends is beyond the scope of this book and such an undertaking could fill a whole library. Here is just a taster of dragons elsewhere.

Mainland Europe

The familiar four-legged, two-winged, fire-snorting dragon is widespread in Europe as is the two-legged, two-winged wyvern. In Scandinavia the limbless worm is known as the lindorm and is the villain of countless legends. It was believed that lindorms grew from ordinary snakes. As the snake grew beyond the norm it took to dwelling in lakes. The growth of a lindorm never stopped but continued throughout its life-span, which unless slain, was virtually indefinite. As the lindorm reached truly fantastic proportions it would leave its lake for the open sea and become a sea serpent. Finally its coils would become so vast that they would drag it to the seabed under its own weight. In Norse mythology the greatest of these serpents was the Jormungander or Midguard serpent. This lindorm was so huge it encircled the whole world in its coils and needed Thor the god of thunder to finally put paid to it. Vast serpents were the adversaries of many gods in many cultures.

In Scandinavia lindorms were believed to encircle churches in their coils and crush them. This seems to hearken back to the dragon as an ancient pagan symbol. In these lands we find another fascinating piece of worm folklore. Towns menaced by a lindorm would often breed a gigantic bull of unnatural size and strength that would be sent out to fight the lindorm. Goring with its horns and stamping with its hooves while its foe bit and constricted with its coils, the fight usually ended in the death of both combatants.

This has interesting modern day analogues. Some of the colossal snakes in South America are known as *mano toro* or the killers of bulls because of their habit of feeding on steers.

Swedish scientist Gunnar Olof Hylten-Cavallius published a book on giant snakes in his country in 1885. In *On the Dragon, Also Called the Lindorm* he published forty-eight verbatim accounts, half involving multiple witnesses. He writes...

> 'In Varend (in southern Sweden) – and probably in other parts of Sweden – a species of giant snakes, called dragons or lindorms, continues to exist. Usually the lindorm is about 10 feet long but specimens of 18 or 20 feet been observed. His body is as thick as a man's thigh; his colour is black with a yellow- flamed belly. Old specimens wear on their necks an integument of long hair or scales, frequently likened to a horse's mane. He has a flat, round or squared head, a divided tongue, and a mouth full of white, shining teeth. His eyes are large and saucer-shaped with a frightfully wild and sparkling stare. His tail is short and stubby and the general shape of the creature is heavy and unwieldy.'

The lindorm has a long pedigree in northern Europe. In 1555 the exiled Archbishop of Upplasa, Olaus Magnus, then residing in Rome, published his book *Historia de Gentibus Sertentrionalibus*. This dealt with the serpentine monsters of Scandinavian waters. He writes:

> 'There is also another serpent of incredible magnitude in a town called Moos [i.e. Lake Mjosa], of the Diocese of Hammer, which as a comet portends change in all the world, so, that portends a change in the kingdom of Norway, as was seen Anno 1522, that lifts himself high above the waters, and rolls himself round like a sphere. This serpent was thought to be fifty cubits long by conjecture, by sight afar off: there followed the banishment of King Christiernus, and the great persecution of the Bishops; and it shew'd also the destruction of the Country.'

We can see from this passage that the Scandinavians held their dragons in as much awe as their Viking ancestors did. The rising himself high and rolling into a sphere sounds like the head and neck aspect and hump aspect of sea and lake monsters.

In 1636 the cleric Nicolas Gramis recorded that a serpent dwelling in the Mjos and Branz River in Norway had left its home and crawled across the surrounding fields. It was said to look like the long mast of a ship and it knocked over trees and huts that stood in its way.

Lindorms, or something very like them, are still reported from deep Scandinavian lakes today. The most famous of these north European beasts lives in Lake Storsjon in Sweden. This is Scandinavia's answer to Loch Ness. On Forson Island there is a huge megalith upon which a lindorm, swallowing its own tail like the orobourus, is carved. Along its coils are written Viking runes. A legend tells that a lindorm is bound to the lake until the runes are deciphered. Deciphered or not a lindorm seems to be resident in Lake Storsjon and has been reported since 1820.

One of the best sightings was made by Martin Olsson, a mechanic at the Ostersund sawmills, lived in a cabin beside the lake.

> 'I was fishing near Forson Island when I got a strange
> feeling someone was watching me. I looked behind
> me and the lake creature was not more than forty
> metres behind my boat. I dropped my pole and line
> in the lake when I saw it. The weather was bright and
> sunny and I got a good view of the animal. The neck
> was long, about as round as a man's body at the base
> where it came up out of the water. It tapered up
> about six feet to a snake like head that was larger
> than what I figured the neck could support. There was
> a hairy fringe just back of the neck, hanging down the
> back. This fringe-like ribbon was stuck close to the
> neck, possibly because of the wetness. The colour was
> greyish brown. The thing had two distinct eyes that
> were reddish in appearance. The body was not
> exactly black but a sort of blackish rust colour in
> appearance. There were a couple of dark humps
> visible beyond the neck. Both of these humps, and the
> part that was out of the water glistened in the

sunlight. I did not see scales. There was a skin on the animal that resembled the skin of a fish.

I didn't want to alarm the animal but I did want to get away as quickly as possible. Moving very cautiously, I took my oars and pulled slowly away from the spot. I became even more frightened when I had rowed about ten metres distance and the animal began to swim towards me. I stopped rowing and the thing just lay there in the water staring at me. This must have gone on for about five minutes. I'm uncertain because my mind was on anything but the passage of time. There was no doubt in my mind that this thing could have overturned my little boat. I thanked God when he dropped beneath the water and I saw a blackish hump move out in the opposite direction.'

A newspaper reporter told his friends how he rowed up to the monster to get a better view of it in 1896.

'At first we thought the dark mass in the water was a boat that had turned over. We observed the mass for a few moments then realised it was the infamous monster of Lake Storsjon. I had just read about the sea-worm mentioned in olden times. I thought this creature could be a throwback to something that once lived in olden days. I talked my companions into rowing out onto the lake where the serpent was making a lot of threshing manoeuvres raising waves and disturbing the calmness of the lake.'

The group observed a smooth-bodied, cinnamon-coloured creature showing several humps above the surface.

Storsjon is not the only Scandinavian lake that has a monster. Lake Seljord in Norway is another hot spot for sightings. According to legend the monster, known as Seljordsorm, once inhabited a smaller mountain lake. It outgrew this abode and moved overland to Lake Seljord. Eiivind Fjodstuft saw it while fishing in 1920. He described it as black, fifty to sixty feet long, with a head like a crocodile.

In the summer of 1975, dentist Rolf Langeland started a practice in a small hamlet called Sandnes close to the lake. Three days after his arrival he was driving near the lake with his three children when they saw Seljordsorm. He brought his car to a halt as five humps broke the surface churning the water and moving at an amazing speed. Langeland estimated the monster to be 30 to 50 metres in length. The size sounds excessive but he may have seen several specimens swimming in line together.

On Easter Monday 1977 Ivar Hesmyr and his daughter Solveig were fishing from a small boat with a neighbour's son. Suddenly three glistening humps rose from the water nearly a hundred metres away. Hesmyr estimated the beast was nine metres long. A serpentine head and neck rose up and the creature began to swim away at a speed that caused the boat to rock. Solveig began screaming and her father attempted to calm her. When he looked up again the Seljordsorm was gone. Solveig said that the humps disappeared first followed by the head and neck. When they reached shore Hesmyr swore he would never go back out on the lake again.

Another, smaller Norwegian lake with a lindorm in residence is Rommen in south-western Norway, close to the Swedish border.

In 1929 Astrid Myrvold was fetching water for her mother when she saw something on the shore. In later life she likened it to a big, black plastic pipe (though these did not exist then). It had a horse-like head and a fin on the tail. Disturbed by her presence it slithered into the lake drawing a large wake behind it. Astrid noticed it had protruding ears or horns. She told her mother but was not believed. Hence she did not speak about it again until 1976 when a local man said he had also seen the monster.

These creatures are not restricted to freshwater. There is a long tradition of sea dragons in Scandinavia. Olaus Magnus's 1555 book, *Historia de Gentibus Serpentrionabilis,* also describes sea monsters in Scandinavian waters. The most infamous was of monstrous size:

> 'They who in Works of Navigation, on the coasts of
> Norway, employ themselves in fishing or merchandise,
> do all agree this strange story. That there is a serpent
> there, which is of vast magnitude, namely 200 foot
> long and moreover 20 foot thick: and is wont to live
> in rocks and caves towards the sea coast about
> Bergen, which will go alone from his holes in a clear
> night, in summer, and devour calves, lambs, and hog,
> or else he goes into the sea to feed on polyps,
> locusts, and all sorts of sea crabs. He hath commonly
> hair hanging from his neck a cubit long, and sharp
> scales, and is black, and he hath flaming shining eyes.

This snake disquiets the shippers, and he puts his
head on high like a pillar, and casteth away men, and
he devours them: and this happeneth not, but it
signifies some wonderfull change of the Kingdom near
at hand: namely the princes shall die, or be banished:
or some tumultuous wars shall presently follow.'

Nearly 200 years later another cleric took up Magnus's reigns and
continued his work. Eric Pontoppidan, Bishop of Bergen, studied
and collected stories of encounters with these creatures, mainly by
fishermen and sailors. The Bishop devoted a whole chapter of his
book *Natural History of Norway* to these monsters, and asked the
question, are they man-eaters?

'I return again to the most interesting inquiry concerning
them, which is whether they do mankind any injury? And
in what manner they may hurt the human species. Arndt
Bernsen, in his Account of the fertility of Denmark and
Norway, p308, affirms that they do; and says that the Sea-
snake, as well as the Trold-whale, often sinks both men
and boats. I have not heard any accounts of such an
accident hereabouts, that might be depended on; but the
North traders inform me of what has frequently happened
to them, namely that a Sea-snakes has raised itself up, and
thrown itself across a boat, and sometimes even across a
vessel of some hundred tons burden, and by its weight has
sunk it down to the bottom. One of the aforesaid North
traders, who says he has been near enough to some of
these Sea-snakes (alive) to feel their smooth skin, informs
me that sometimes they will raise up their frightful heads,
and snap a man out of a boat without hurting the rest...

It is said that they will sometimes fling themselves in a
wide circle around a boat, so that the men are surrounded
on all sides. This Snake, I observed before, generally
appears on the water in folds or coils: and the fishermen,
in a known custom in that case, never row towards the
openings, or those places were the body is not seen, but is
concealed under the water, if they did that the snake
would raise itself up and upset the boat. On the contrary,
they row full against the highest part that is visible, which
makes the snake immediately dive; and they are released
from their fears.'

One of the most dramatic encounters took place in 1894, during an exceptionally hot July. Two sea serpents blockaded the isolated fishing village of Ervinken in Norway, close to the border with Finland. The newspaper *Finmarkeposten* reported that the town's residents came down to watch the sea serpents swimming back and forth in front of the harbour's entrance. Several fishermen admitted that they had never seen anything so big in their voyages. The newspaper went on:

> 'The sea serpent was dark yellow in colour, had a round body, and a length of at least 180 feet. It moved very fast through the water with serpentine coils. The head was about the size of a barrel, but rather more pointed in front, and immediately behind it the creature had a large ring situated between the head and the body, which seemed to be smooth and without fins.'

A whaling vessel from Hammerfest had met up with three crews from fishing ships and who had come into port babbling in terror about giant snakes. The whaler had set out to engage the monsters but they had vanished by the time it arrived.

In Finland dragons are called Lappalainen Luppakorva. They live on the Arctic hills of Lapland. In colour the Lappalainen Luppakorva is said to be black, neon green or sometimes something in between. They only eat fat people and hate eggs, so if you eat eggs at night then you don't have to worry about being eaten by dragons.

The dragons of ancient Greece seemed to have been serpentine. Indeed we get the word 'python' from the dragon slain by the young Apollo with arrows of lightning. Greek dragons often dwelt in tombs and temples. The dragon that guarded the golden fleece at Cholcis was said to never sleep and be ever watchful. Snakes have no eyelids and are hence 'ever watchful'. The third century Greek author Aelian writes in his *De Natura Animalium* of them being kept in sacred groves and being ministered to by virgins. It is possible they were actually real pythons brought to Greece from India.

Not all dragons were huge. The tiny basilisk was well-known throughout Europe. In Rome during the reign of Pope Leo X a basilisk was captured and blamed for an outbreak of plague. Another was said to lurk in a well in Vienna and killed people with its pestilent breath. It was discovered in 1202. In 1587 a specimen was killed in a cellar in Warsaw after causing the death of several locals. It turned out to be a disappointingly small snake. The others were also probably harmless snakes found in areas where sulphur or methane fumes had built up to dangerous levels or natural diseases had broken out.

The basilisk has not entirely been banished into limbo. When the Spanish conquistadors first began to explore South America they discovered a large lizard. It was bright green and bore a rooster-like crest on its head. They naturally called it a basilisk. *Basiliscus basiliscus* to give it its Latin name (there are in fact several related species) lacks its legendary counterpart's baleful stare but it has a power almost as incredible. When alarmed this 60 centimetre (2 foot) lizard rears onto its hind legs and runs across the surface of rivers. Its elongated toes splay out to spread its body weight. As long as it runs quickly it does not break the surface tension. Hence it is sometimes known as the Jesus Christ lizard.

An altogether more deadly 'modern basilisk' story may exist much closer to home. In the forests outside Saint Petersburg is said to lurk a deadly snake that has a crest like a rooster's comb. A number of people are killed by its bite each year. The venom is said to cause madness followed by death. Symptoms include eating dirt, fever, hallucinations and stripping off clothes. The victims are often found naked. No scientist has ever examined a specimen but to the local people it is just another woodland animal.

The salamander was a tiny dragon that possessed death-dealing powers out of all proportion to its size. It was no more than 30 centimetres (one foot) in length and shaped like a lizard. Its body was covered in star-shaped markings. The salamander could live in naked flame without the slightest harm to itself. It was also highly poisonous, spitting a foul foam from its mouth. This caused its victim's hair to fall out and their skin to wither before death. The only animal immune to its venom was the pig. Pigs could eat salamanders with immunity but if humans were to then eat the flesh of the pig they would die due to the venom accumulated in the swine's fat.

The power of the salamander's toxin was truly immense. Should a salamander enter a pool the water therein would be poisoned indefinitely. Alexander the Great was said to have lost 2,000 horses and 4,000 soldiers when they drank from a stream that a salamander had crawled through. It was also believed that if a salamander came into contact with wood used for a baker's fire then the bread would be contaminated.

Another strange quirk of the salamander was that it was supposed to be able to spin itself a cocoon out of a fireproof wool-like substance. This became known as salamander's wool. This fireproof wool was much sought after. Pope Alexander III was said to possess his own tunic of salamander's wool. The Byzantine Emperor Manual Comnenus was said to have received a letter from the semi-mythical Prester John, a priest king who ruled over a mysterious land some now believe to be Ethiopia. In the letter Prester John speaks of salamanders and how their wool is gathered and spun into cloth. When in need of cleaning, garments made from the wool were cast into flames.

Like the basilisk the salamander has passed on its name to a modern successor. A group of harmless amphibians, most notably the European fire salamander (*Salamandra salamandra*), a striking black and yellow species. The lethal poison that could find its way into bread if the baker used wood that a salamander had crawled across may have its genesis in rye ergot, a form of fungus that can grow in flour. If ingested rye ergot in bread could cause allergic reactions and be lethally poisonous. In France in 922 40,000 people died of rye ergot poisoning and in 1128 14,000 died in Paris alone.

A less deadly but equally amazing relative of the salamander was the pyrallis. This was the very smallest kind of dragon, being no larger than a fly. It was bronze in colour with four legs, insect-like wings and a reptilian head. The pyrallis was found only in the copper smelting forges and foundries of Cyprus. Whole swarms of them would dance around inside forges like living sparks, but should they leave the flames they would cool and die.

The Middle East

Persian dragons fall half-way between Western and Eastern dragons. They have the ornate, elongated look of Eastern dragons but the savage nature of Western dragons. Their wings are usually feathery rather than bat-like. A whole dynasty of Persian heroes slew dragons. The most famous story involved Rustam who was attacked in the desert by a dragon that coiled about him. His loyal horse Rakhsh bit and kicked at the coils until the dragon loosened its grip

Opposite: *Persian dragon by Ian Brown*

and attacked the horse. This gave the hero Rustam the opportunity to draw his sword and slay it.

Other Middle Eastern dragons were more serpentine. Around 250 BC at the time of the first Punic War (264–241), Rome was embroiled in a prolonged struggle with the city of Carthage (near where modern day Tunis stands) over the control of Sicily. General Marcus Atilius Regulus led his army towards the city when he came to the River Baradas. A titanic serpent rose up from the reed beds. The men fell back in horror and after some consultation decided to cross the river further up stream. But as the soldiers began to ford the waters the monster reappeared and seized a man. As each of the warriors tried to cross he was snatched by the beast's massive jaws, encircled in its coils and dragged under.

After many men were lost in this way, and it seemed as if the serpent would defeat the entire army, Regulus ordered that the giant snake should be bombarded with *ballistae* – giant, rock hurling catapults. *Ballistae* were trained on the creature and it gradually began to retreat under the bombardment. One boulder struck the giant's skull with fatal force and the monster snake collapsed onto the bank.

The soldiers dragged the vast corpse onto the bank and measured it. It was an astounding 36 metres! The jaws and skin were sent back to Rome as a trophy where it was on public display in a temple on Capitol Hill until 133 BC when it was lost during the Numantine war with the Iberian Celts. Regulus himself was granted an ovation.

Arficanus Leo (Hasan ibn Muhhammad al Wazzan al Fasi) was a traveller and writer born in Granada in 1485. He was enslaved by European pirates but freed by Pope Leo X. He travelled widely in Africa and visited Timbuktu twice. His were the first descriptions of the city to find their way to Europe. He wrote of huge venomous dragons inhabiting the Atlas Mountains in North Africa. Events in the twentieth century may support his claims.

In 1958, Belkhouriss Abd el-Khader, an Algerian who served in the French army at Beni Ounif, Algeria, was attacked and bitten by a thirteen-metre long snake. The snake was killed and its skin preserved but has since been lost.

The following year a fantastical story, a sequel to Regulus's adventure, occurred near a garrison in Ain Sefra, Algeria. A monster snake that had just swallowed a whole camel was captured in a trench filled with branches by nomads. A French battalion, the Twenty-Sixth Dragoons were brought in to kill it. Their carbine rifles did little damage and they had to finish the monster with machine guns. The beast was 36 metres long, the same size as Regulus' reptile, and bore a one-metre crest on its head. No one seems to know what became of the body.

In early January 1967 a nine metre snake was seen on the construction site of the Djorf-Torba dam, east of Bechar, Algeria. A worker called Hamaza Rhamani wedged it against some rocks with his bulldozer. He reported that the beast's fangs were some 60 millimetres long. Later that year, in the same area Rhamani saw another specimen. He followed its trail to some barrels of oil from which, bizarrely, it seemed to have been drinking. He saw the snake coiled in the shadow of a pile of crushed rocks. He estimated the length to be five to seven metres.

The Orient

Asia is filled with dragons. They differ from their western counterparts in several ways. Most importantly they were thought of as benevolent creatures, friendly to mankind if treated with respect. This is in stark contrast to their European brethren. Eastern dragons were associated more with the element of water than that of fire. They made their lairs in deep pools, lakes, rivers and seas. The breath of the dragon condensed to form rain. Dragons were believed to control rainfall and the weather in general. They also controlled the seas and rivers. If offended they could cause flooding or drought.

In China the dragon went through a complex life cycle taking 3,000 years to complete. Interestingly at various stages of their changing morphology they resemble different kinds of western dragon. Dragon eggs were said to resemble jewels and when the dragons hatched from them they looked like diminutive and unimpressive water snakes (much like the deadly basilisk). After 500 years the tiny reptile would grow into a gargantuan snake with a carp-like head. In this phase the dragon was known as a *kiao* and resembled the huge lindorms of Europe. It stays like this for a further 1,000 years until it develops a reptilian head and four legs. In this form it is called a *lung*. This guise lasts 500 years until the dragon grows branching horns and becomes a *khoi lung*, the best-known form of Chinese dragon. Another millennium brings forth fan-like wings in the

dragon's adult stage. Then it is known as a *ying lung* or true dragon and resembles an ornate, elongated form of the Western firedrake or true dragon.

One particular *ying lung* was the Responding Dragon. His job was to kill gods who got out of hand. The Responding Dragon killed Chi You, the god of war at Cruelplough Earthmound after Chi You had waged war on the Yellow God, the dragon's ally.

The Chinese dragon's appearance was detailed by the scholar Wang Fu of the Han dynasty of 206 BC to AD 220. According to his writings the dragon possessed the head of a camel, the eyes of a daemon, the ears of a cow, the neck of a snake, the antlers of a deer, the feet of a tiger and the claws of an eagle. Dragons generally had four claws on each foot. The exception was the Imperial dragon that had five claws; only the Emperor of China was allowed to use the iconography of this dragon. Any one else who dared to use it could be put to death.

The male dragon was said to have a magical pearl imbedded in the skin under its chin or in its head. Many serpents and dragons were believed to bear such gems in their skulls much like the pearls in oysters.

Dragon bones (or *lung ku*) and dragon teeth (or *lung chhi*) have been used in the cornucopia of Chinese folk medicine for thousands of years. The *Pan Taso Kang Mu* is a book written in late sixteenth or early seventeenth century (Ming Period) China. It collects together fragments of much older works and contains many references to dragon bones.

The *Pieh luh* is one of these older works. It tells us that different types and parts of dragon bones have differing powers, attributes and efficacy. The dragon's spine is the most sought after part of the skeleton. The dragon's 'brain' is preserved as 'white earth' and was also of great value. It was believed to cure ailments of the tongue. It could be that this white earth or dragon's brain is in fact asbestos. This same substance was known as salamander's wool in the west.

The smaller bones marked with wider lines were believed to be female and the larger bones with narrower lines were male. Bones of variegated colour were the most effective and esteemed. Yellow or flesh-coloured bones were of medium value and black bones

Opposite: *Eastern dragon by Ian Brown.*

inferior. If the bones were gathered by a woman, says the book, they should not be used!

The colours of dragon bones also relate to the internal organs that the bones were thought to affect as medicine: Blue equated to the liver and gall, red corresponded with the heart and large intestine, while yellow was associated with the spleen and stomach.

The dragon/water link is also found in the unearthing of dragon bones. Joseph Needham in *Science and Civilisation in China* records the digging of an irrigation canal between the rivers of Lo and Shang-ye around 133 BC (Han Period). Many dragon bones were uncovered during the digging. So many in fact that the canal was named 'Dragon-Head Waterway'. Fifty years later the writer Wang Chung records that dragon bones had been found after the control of a flood. Doubtless the large bones of extinct animals would occasionally be washed from their earth prisons by floodwaters thereby strengthening the belief that dragons controlled waterways, seas and the weather. A dragon developing into a new stage of life and casting off its old bones with its old skin would naturally cause such a disturbance.

Modern day reports of dragons are more common in Asia than anywhere else on Earth. In late July 2002 an astounding report of what must be the greatest mass sighting of a dragon filtered out of China. Lake Tianchi or Celestial Lake lies in Jinlin province on the border of north-east China and North Korea. It is the bowl of an extinct volcano covering 9.8 square kilometres and 373 metres deep. There is a long tradition of the lake being the lair of a dragon and before the Cultural Revolution it was known as Dragon Lake.

On the 25 July a black, elongated creature, with a horned, horse-like head broke the surface only ten metres from the shore. The animal was visible for ten minutes and leaped from the water on several occasions. Five hundred people witnessed the dragon's appearance including a party of two hundred tourists who were climbing the Changbai Mountains. One of these apparently caught the beast on film.

The sightings spawned a forty-minute documentary on the Huichin TV channel. The programme showed film and photographs of the creature taken over the years and recounted some of the thousands of eyewitness accounts, mainly from mountaineers reaching back to the 1900s.

On 18 August 1901, First Officer F. Wolfe in charge of the Chinese customs launch *Lung-tsing* was off Tai Yue Shan Island, Hong Kong. He spotted a dragon-like animal coiled on the sea's surface. It held its head about a metre above the water. It bore a crest on its head and two fins high on its neck. He ordered his second officer, V. Kuster, into a gig with a number of sailors and (stupidly) commanded them to attempt to kill it with a boat hook. This seems to me akin to attempting to knock over Nelson's Column with a fly whisk. In any event the serpent bit at one of the oars and reared up three metres out of the water before diving and vanishing. The men estimated its length at twelve to fifteen metres.

Another series of sightings had occurred in Along Bay, Vietnam four years previously. *Long* is another spelling of *lung*. The French gunboat *Avalanche* several times encountered dragon-like creatures in this island-dotted bay on the coast off Tongking. The first was on July 1897. Lieutenant Lagresill takes up the story:

'In the month of July last [1897] the *Avalanche* saw for the first time, off Along Bay two animals of weird shape and large dimensions; their length was reckoned at about 65 feet and their diameter 6 to 10 feet. The feature of these animals was that their body was not rigid like that of known cetaceans, but made undulatory movements similar to a snake's, but in a vertical direction. A revolving gun was loaded and fired at 600 yards, at slightly too short range. They immediately dived, breathing loudly and leaving a wash on the surface like breakers. They did not reappear, but we thought we saw their heads, which we judged to be of small dimensions.

On February 12th of this year (1898) when crossing the Bay of Fai-tsi-long, I saw similar animals again. At once I gave chase and had the revolving guns loaded. Several shots were fired at one of them, at ranges of between 300 and 400 yards, and the last two shots reached them without seeming to do them the least harm, the shells bursting on the surface. I also tried to reach them with the bow of the ship, but their speed was greater than that of the *Avalanche*. Each time, however, that this animal came into shallow water it turned back, which enabled me to gain upon it and confirm its great size. It frequently emerged, and always one noticed its undulatory movements. Each emergence was preceded by a jet of water, or rather of water vapour made by a loud breath...

The colour of the animal was grey with several black fins. Its trail was easily followed by the release of its breath, which formed circles 4 to 5 yards in diameter on the surface of the sea, which was then perfectly calm. At one moment I thought I had reached it. The chase went on for an hour and a half and had to be abandoned as night was falling.'

The animals were reported in the same area for the next six years.

The strong belief in dragons among the Chinese is illustrated by the next encounter.

The steamer *Saint Francois-Xanier* was on the Tongking to New Caledonia, Australia run when she encountered a sea dragon. Her captain Raoul Jaillard recorded the sighting:

'Haipong, 18 March 1925

Sir, I am sending you a little sketch drawn at sea several minutes after the appearance of the famous sea serpent. The second captain, the second lieutenant, the radio officer, and the third engineer are unanimous in confirming the following lines:

On 2nd February 1925 while on passage from Noumea to Newcastle, the ship was making 10 knots, at 18.30 hours abeam of Port Stephens on the east coast of Australia, two masses like turtle's shells were seen floating 30 feet from the ship on the starboard bow.

Abeam of the engines there rose a big head like a camel's head, on a long flexible neck having a great similarity to a swan's neck. The height of the neck was about eight feet. The body, thick as the big Bordeaux barrels, formed a chain of five loops; on the fourth loop, an aileron as on sharks of large dimensions, measuring five feet in height and in width at the base. The aileron seemed to be black in colour;

the colour of the animal was dirty yellow, the skin smooth without appearance of scales.

As it passed astern of the ship and was abeam of the starboard screw, the animal's head began to move backwards and forwards, which led us to think it had been touched by a blade of the screw; its movement seemed hindered and it was not at all like that of the very little snakes seen near the coast.

The animal was visible for fifteen minutes, no optical illusion is possible. For besides the testimony of the Europeans, the Blacks from New Caledonia serving as seamen on board, the Annamite boys and the Chinese stokers all gave one cry: 'There is the Dragon!'. The Chinese even made an offering to it.

As night falls very quickly at that time of year we could not give other details, being one and all fairly taken aback by this fantastic apparition...

Raoul Jaillard'

During the Manchuria regime in August, 1944, a black dragon fell to the ground at the Chen family's Weizi Village, about 9.4 miles north-west of Zhaoyuan County, on the south shore of the Mudan River (the old name of a section of Songhua River) in Heilongjiang province. The black dragon was on the verge of death. The eyewitness said that this creature had a horn on its head, scales covering its body, and had a strong fishy smell that attracted numerous flies.

More recently a photograph was taken from an aeroplane above Tibet that alleges to show two dragons in flight. On 22 June 2004, the photographer went to Tibet's Amdo region to attend the Qinghai to Xizang railroad-laying ceremony, and then took a plane from Lhasa to fly back inland. When flying over the Himalayas, he accidentally caught these two 'dragons' in a picture that he took. He called these two objects 'the Tibet dragons.'

The picture shows what seem to be parts of two large serpentine objects coiling through the clouds.

Japanese dragons were called *tatsu*. They were similar to Chinese dragons in their looks but bore only three claws on each foot. In Japan dragons were not as closely linked to rainfall as their Chinese relatives. The dwelt in mountains, lakes, rivers and most importantly the sea. Dragons could control the abundance of fish and the catches of fishermen. Angry dragons could cause earthquakes and those who lived in the sea could send tsunami, giant waves that could destroy whole towns.

Like Chinese dragons, Japanese dragon eggs resembled huge jewels. But unlike the lengthy life cycle of the Chinese dragon, Japanese dragons reached adult size very quickly. They hatched from small holes in the top of the eggs and emerged as little snakes. But upon wriggling free they grow almost instantly into gigantic dragons. One story told of a peasant boy who brought home some gems he had found near a river. They were in fact dragon eggs that hatched out into massive flying reptiles that smashed the roof off his house.

Later in life dragons may grow wings. These tend to be bird-like as opposed to the bat-like wings of Western dragons or the fan-like wings of Chinese dragons. In this form they are called *hai riyo.*

Lake Ikeda near the city of Kagoshuma on the Island of Kyushu has a latter-day dragon. Witnesses describe a hump-backed beast with a snaky head and neck. Several photographs have been taken of the Ikeda dragon. The first was in 1978 by Mr Toksiaki Matsuhara. He was a folklorist investigating the stories attached to the lake. On December 16th he saw a whirlpool form in the centre of the lake and watched it through his telescope. Later he saw a pair of creatures together close to Metow-Iwa (Married Couple) Rocks and photographed them. The shots appear to show the two animals together, their humps creating waves. The monster has been christened 'Issie'.

Many respectable people have seen Issie, including the president of a construction firm. Yutaka Kawaji and twenty members of his family saw a black-skinned animal showing six to nine metres of its body above the surface. Mr Kawaji pursued the monster in his motorboat. It dived and resurfaced several times.

Iamu Horiouchi says the thing he saw in the lake was a row of humps 20 metres long. He took eight photos of the phenomena on the 4th October 1978, but none came out clearly.

A mere four hours later coffee shop owner Hiromi Nakahama watched for nearly four minutes as two massive humps rose and fell in the waters.

Issie has counterparts in other areas of Japan. Also on Kyushu is Lake Toya, home of a similar entity. On the northern island of Hokkaido lies Lake Kutcharo, home to a monster called 'Kussie'. Local people have formed a protection society for the animal.

Winged dragons are known from Japan as well. In May 2003 David Nardiello was working teaching English in Nigshimozu high school in the town of Watagh Shinke-Cho, Osaka, Japan. He was cycling home late one night through heavy rain. The torrent had formed a pool in some nearby rice fields. Nardiello saw a white animal emerge from the water and turn to look at him. It had a long neck and snake-like head with black 'shark eyes' and fangs. The body and tail were akin to a lizard while the four legs resembled a cat. The animal had leathery, featherless wings. It flew into the air to a height of 30 metres and Nardiello, increasingly scared, cycled home as fast as he could.

Later that night he saw it flying through the night sky from his third-storey flat. He asked his neighbours if they had seen it but none had. Some however said they had heard weird cries from the fields for the past few nights. His co-worker Kato Sensi dubbed it *Nekohebitori* or 'cat-snake-bird'. Nardiello felt strongly that the animal was a predator and was dangerous.

In Indo-China dragons tend to be identical to those in China. The are called *long* rather than *lung*. The exception is in Thailand, which seems to share its dragon lore with India. In both countries the dragon is known as the *naga*. Nagas tend to be limbless but have the distinct eastern dragon's head. Like other Oriental dragons they lair in water and have control over this element. Nagas could take human form but usually retained the serpent tail while in this guise. Nagas could be good or evil.

I have investigated reports of such beasts in October 2000 (the Chinese year of the dragon!) searched the caves, rivers and forests of Thailand for nagas and heard some amazing eyewitness accounts. I visited the village of Phon Pisai and spoke with a Buddhist abbot and his monks about a strange naga encounter. The temple was the most spectacular building in the village, adorned with dragons and nagas.

Eight years before there was an old temple where the fine new one stands. The ancient, tumbledown erection had become unsightly and dangerous so it was decided to pull it down and build a new one.

But whenever workmen approached a huge black snake would appear and rear up striking at them.

Workmen, monks, and abbot all saw it. It was very thick but they could not estimate the length as the creature never revealed its whole body but kept most of its coils in the building. Finally an offering was given to the monster and it disappeared overnight.

Another witness was Officer Suphat who is Chief of Police in Phon Piasi. Three years previously he and a group of thirty people had been walking on some cliffs overlooking the Mekong. They had seen what at first they believed to be flotsam floating along in the river. As it drew closer they became aware that it was moving against the current.

Looking down they saw a gigantic black snake swimming with a horizontal flexation, indicative of a fish, amphibian or reptile.

I asked Officer Suphat how long the monster was. His answer staggered me – seventy metres! I double-checked thinking there had been a mistranslation but he clarified seventy metres or two hundred and thirty feet.

The crowd watched as the naga swam by, then were overcome by fear and fled. He later asked a Buddhist monk about his sighting. The holy man confirmed what he had seen was a naga. He explained that some years ago a statue of Buddha was being transported by boat across the river. The boat capsized and the statue fell to the riverbed. Since then nagas have come to protect it.

The officer's monster seems excessively long. I think what he may have seen were several nagas swimming in line, perhaps males in pursuit of a female. Alternatively it could have been a long wake that made an already huge serpent seem even longer.

Mr Pimpa, an old man from a remote jungle village took me deep into a network of caves to an underground river where he had seen a naga some ten years before. We travelled for about a mile until we came to the place Mr Pimpa had seen the monster some ten years ago. It was an elongated tubular cave. The old man had been exploring by candlelight when he had turned into this cave and come across a giant snake. Its head was in the shadows but the visible portion of its body was twenty metres long. Mr Pimpa pressed himself back against the wall in terror as the giant reptile crawled by at an agonizingly slow pace. Its scales were black with a glossy green sheen and it was around 75 to 90 centimetres thick.

Finally it disappeared along the passage and Mr Pimpa collapsed gasping in relief. In the dark his had fell against a tiny semi-precious stone, which he pocketed. Scrambling back out of the cave system he returned to the village and told his weird tale. He later had the stone mounted onto a serpent-shaped ring, which he showed to us. He believed that despite the fear he felt at the time the naga brought him luck. Prior to his adventure he was a poor man who could hardly afford to feed his family. After it he inherited some land and became a successful farmer. The caves were now considered sacred to the villagers.

I came away convinced in the existence of some kind of huge reptile unknown to science lurking in the primal morasses of Indo-China.

The naga has reared its head in other parts of Asia as well. In 1966 a peasant digging in the mud on the bank of the Mekong, close to the Lan Xang hotel in Vientiane, the capital of Laos, uncovered some huge white eggs. Subsequently he claimed that the naga appeared to him in a dream demanding the return of its eggs and threatening to flood the river if they were not given back. He took them to General Kong Le, leader of the Neutralist army. The general showed the eggs to Premier Prince Souvana Phouma and warned him of the impending peril. Le was to lead the people in a ceremony of atonement but the Prince was unimpressed by the peasant fairy tales. The ceremony was never carried out and the monsoon rains brought a huge flood to the city. Tragically no one knows what happened to the naga eggs.

Back in Thailand a strikingly similar event was recorded in May 1980. Fisherman Prancha Pongpaew found seventeen eggs in the River Ping, north Thailand. The eggs were the size of watermelons and seemed to be linked. He brought five of them to the surface and took them back to Songhtam village. The eggs were broken but they smelled so bad that they were thrown to dogs who ran away in fear.

That night the villagers were awoken by an odd wailing sound and were horrified to see two black serpents the size of palm trees with crested heads rearing up out of the river. The following night a religious ceremony was performed on the banks of the river but the nagas did not reappear.

It should be noted that snakes either lay eggs on land or give birth to live young. The strand of linked eggs in water is very odd and distinctly un-reptilian. They sound like out-sized toad spawn.

Perhaps the nagas and the eggs were two unconnected events.

The year previously a naga had caused a stir in Malaysia when it turned up in a disused mining pool in Semenyih. Fisherman Lebai Ramli saw it rise up from the water and fled in terror. The incident caused a local stir as crowds of people, some armed, swarmed to the pool to try and see the monster. Signboards were put up telling people the way to the pool and there was even an ice cream man on hand! Amazingly the naga obliged. It surfaced at about 12.30 when many witnesses saw a creature with a head the size of a scooter wheel. Farmer Enick Arshad described seeing a log like creature swimming three to five metres from the bank.

Enick Jaafar's twelve-year old son claimed to have seen a snake-like animal with a head the size of an oil drum held 60 centimetres above the water. Enick himself saw the creature shortly after the Second World War. He described it as a snake the size of a tree trunk. The monster was held responsible for the disappearance of two buffaloes and other local livestock.

In 2004 I was in the Indonesian island of Sumatra searching for an undiscovered species of upright walking ape called orang-pendek. I met with and spoke to the Kubu tribe, a jungle tribe with little contact with Western culture. The chief, Nylam, and his warriors had seen orang-pendek but they also insisted they had seen gigantic snakes bearing horns like those of an ox. They called these giant snakes nagas. The Kubu believed that eventually the great horned snakes change into huge crocodiles. The folklore of these people is poorly studied and, to my knowledge, this is the first time anyone has written it down.

Africa

The cradle of man is home to a number of different kinds of dragon. In the swamps of the Sudan is said to live a giant serpent dragon known as the *lau*. Natives describe the beast as twelve to thirty metres long, about as thick as a donkey and yellow in colour. Some descriptions furnish it with a crest or mane (a curious appendage for a snake but one seen in several areas). Strangely it is also said to possess facial tentacles with which it grabs its prey (another recurring motif is horns or tentacles on the head).

The folklore attached to this monster is singularly bizarre. If the *lau* sees a human before he sees it the man will die. Conversely if the man sees the *lau* first it will be the serpent that expires.

The 1920s explorer and naturalist J.G. Millans interviewed a Westerner who firmly believed in the monster. Sergeant Stephens (who was never identified with a first name) told him:

'One Abriahim Mohamed, in the employ of the company [a telegraph company], saw a lau killed near Raub, at a village called Bogga. The man I knew and closely questioned. He always repeated the same description of the monstrous reptile. More recently one was killed by some Shilluks at Koro-a-ta beyond Jebel-Zeraf (Addar Swamps). I obtained some of the neck bones of this example from a Shilluk who was wearing them as a charm. These I sent to Deputy-Governor Jackson (now of Dongola province), who in turn sent them to the British Museum for identification, but no satisfactory explanation was given, nor was it suggested what species of snake they could belong to.'

Abriahim's story of the size and shape of the great reptile was corroborated by one Rabha Ringbi, a Nian-Niam from the neighbourhood of Wau in the Bahr-el-Ghazal, who had seen a similar monster killed in swamps near that place.

'Dinkas living at Kilo [a telegraph station on the Zeraf] told me that the lau frequents the great swamp in the neighbourhood of that station and they occasionally hear its loud booming cry at night.

A short time ago I met a Belgian administrator at Rejaf. He had just come back from the Congo, and said he was convinced of the existence of the lau as he had seen one of these great serpents in a swamp and fired at it several times, but his bullets had no effect. He also stated that the monster made a huge trail in the swamp as it moved into deeper water.'

Another intriguing piece of evidence was photographed by Captain William Hitchins and published in the magazine *Discovery*. This was a wooden ritual mask of the beast. When Hitchins questioned Meshengu she Gunda, the native singer and sculptor who made the mask, as to the beast's existence the African replied philosophically:

'I might have said, as a young man, when I was ignorant, that there was no such thing as a motor car. I had never seen or even heard of one then. But there

is your motor car in the sight of my eyes and I have
sat on its chairs and heard its bowels digest inside it.
It is thus of the lau.'

An unknown species of African snake bears an uncanny
resemblance to the basilisk. The crested crowing cobra is reported
from central and southern Africa. This reptile is said to be 6 metres
(20 feet) long and grey or brown in colour. It has a scarlet crest like
a rooster's comb on its head as well as a pair of red wattles. Its
cockerel-like attributes do not end there. The creature makes a noise
very like a cock's crowing, hence its name. It is said to be arboreal
and highly venomous. Hyraxes seem to be its favoured prey. It also
attacks humans by lunging from overhanging braches and biting
their faces. Some natives, when walking through forested areas,
carry pots of boiling water on their heads to scald the attacking
creature.

Dr J.O. Shircore obtained some remains of a crested crowing cobra
in 1944. A witch doctor in Malawi gave him a plate of bone from
the crest with skin still attached and several vertebrae and neck
bones from at least two specimens.

In a 1962 letter to the publication *African Wild Life* John Knott
recounts his brush with what may be the same species. While
driving home from Binga in the Kariba area of Zimbabwe (then
southern Rhodesia) in May 1959 he ran over a 2 metre long black
snake. Upon investigation he discovered that the reptile had a
symmetrical crest on its head. The crest could be erected by way of
five internal prop-like structures.

Mokele-mbembe is a giant reptile said to inhabit the swamps of the
Congo, perhaps the most formidable jungle on Earth. Its name
means 'he who dams the river' on account of its size. Brown in
colour with a long neck and tail the beast is said to be aggressive
and to destroy canoes that come too close. There have been many
accounts of the monster, too many to repeat here so I will only give
you a couple of the more dramatic accounts.

James Powell, member of the crocodile specialist group of the
International Union for Conservation of Nature and Natural
Resources investigated reports. Pascal Moteka, a pygmy who lived
near Lake Tele (infamous for sightings), recounted to Powell of a
killing of a Mokele-mbembe shortly before his birth (around 1950).

The fishermen were too afraid of going out onto Lake Tele because of the monsters which entered it via waterways or *molibos*. The tribe's men cut down some trees of about fifteen centimetres in diameter and trimmed off the branches. Then they sharpened one end of each and rammed the blunt ends into the mud at the bottom of one of the waterways to form a barrier against the monster. One of the creatures tried to smash its way through and while entangled on the spikes the pygmies managed to spear it to death.

There was a great celebration and the animal's carcass was butchered and eaten. However all who ate the flesh of the *Mokele-mbembe* were poisoned and died soon afterwards. This recalls the almost universal belief in the toxicity of dragon blood. In many British dragon legends so much as a drop may be lethal and many victorious heroes met their end by spilling the blood of their terrible foes. This tale was latter confirmed by other fishermen in the area.

Pascal had seen the animals himself, mainly in mid-morning. He related seeing their long necks rise two metres from the water and on occasion a rounded back surfacing like a buoy. His intense fear of the creatures prevented him from approaching them and consequently he only observed them from a distance.

Other witnesses saw the animal at much closer range. Nicolas Mondogo said his father had seen a massive animal with a long neck come out of the river and onto a sandbank. It left dinner plate-sized tracks and a great furrow where its tail had dragged in the wet sand. This occurred between the villages of Mokengi and Bandeko on the upper Likouala-aux-Herbes River. Close to this spot Nicolas had his own sighting when aged seventeen. It was seven a.m. and he was on his way to a Catholic mission at Bandeko. He had paused to hunt some monkeys when a huge animal rose from the river. The water in the area was only one metre deep so he could observe the underbelly and legs of the animal. The beast stayed in view for three minutes. It had a long neck as thick as a man's thigh, a head that bore a comb like a rooster, and was reddish brown in colour. It was a mere twelve metres away and was some ten metres long. It stood two metres high and possessed a neck of a similar length, giving a height of approximately four metres, quite comparable to a giraffe. The tail seemed longer than the neck.

David Mambamlo, a schoolteacher saw it even closer. Only three years ago he had been canoeing just upstream from Epena at about three p.m. when a two metre head and neck broke the surface only ten metres from his vessel. He was mesmerised with horror as it rose further out of the river exposing its upper breast. The monster was grey in colour with no visible scales. David picked out a picture of an *Apatasaurus* from a book and said that the animal most resembled that. He subsequently showed the expedition the location of his sighting, a cave in the riverbank one kilometre from the village. The water level had dropped revealing the cave but no occupant was spied.

The Congo dragon is believed by some to be a surviving descendant of the sauropod dinosaurs. I think it is much more likely to be a gigantic semi-aquatic monitor lizard.

In his book *In Witch-bound Africa*, Frank H. Melland describes the beliefs of the Bokaonde and Kaode people of the swamps of northern Zimbabwe (Rhodesia back then in the 1920s). He told of a frightening winged beast called the *kongamato* or 'overwhelmer of boats'. It was said to swoop down and overturn boats as they tried to cross rivers in the swamps. The natives had charms to ward the monster off. The *kongamato*, they said, had the power to cause the waters to rise swamping the vessels. Others claimed it actually dived into the water and turned the boats over. Once more we can note the association of dragons with the control of water. In 1911 two women were killed in a flash flood. This was said to be the work of the *kongamato*. The charm consisted of the root of the mulendi tree ground up and mixed with water until it becomes a paste. This is then put into a cup and carried on their canoes. When crossing a ford on foot strips of the root are carried in a bundle. The bundle was dipped in the water should the monster appear. Some said that even to look upon the *kongamato* meant death. The horror was thought to be flesh and blood rather than a spirit but none the less it was deemed immortal and unkillable. Victims of the *kongamato* would have their little toes and fingers eaten together with their eyes, nose and ear lobes.

The natives described it as a sort of bird without feathers and possessing a beak with teeth. Melland, realising the implications, questioned them further. The *kongamato* had a wingspan of over two metres, leathery red skin, and bat-like wings. It lived in the Jinundu swamps, a five hundred square kilometre morass of marsh, fern, tree, and creeper. When showing them a picture of a pterosaur in a book the natives excitedly identified it as the *kongamato*. Melland considered that it might be a surviving *Pterodactyl* and searched in for the monster without success. No native would be his guide in the feared Jinudu.

English newspaper correspondent G. Ward Price was accompanying the soon-to-be Duke of Windsor on an official trip to Rhodesia in 1925. They visited a local civil servant. A foolhardy native had braved the cursed swamps and later reappeared with a gaping wound in his chest. He was taken to the house of the civil servant and told his uncanny tale. While in the swamps he was attacked by a huge bird-like creature that stabbed at him with a long, murderous beak. The civil servant (who, it seems had heard similar accounts) showed him a book on prehistoric animals. On seeing pictures of pterosaurs the native ran from the house screaming.

In the West a ghostly, ethereal globe of light bobbing and flitting in the inky night sky would doubtless be called a UFO and some would even deem it an alien craft. To the Namaqua people of Namibia this light would mean something infinitely more terrifying, a latter-day dragon. The Namaqua have been reporting such creatures for decades. Their flying snake is described as being the size of a large python, yellow in colour and speckled with brown. From its cranium two horns sprout and a pair of bat-like wings grow from behind the head. Strangest of all a glowing ball of light is said to shine on its forehead. This is strikingly reminiscent of the magical pearls or jewels that were said to be embedded in the heads of Asian dragons. It would be easy to dismiss this as native folklore but white settlers have seen them as well. In January 1942 sixteen-year old Michael Esteruise was tending sheep when something emerged from a cave on top of a nearby hill and launched an attack.

> 'I heard a sound like wind blowing through a pipe, and suddenly the snake came flying through the air at me... it landed with a thud and I threw myself out of its path. The snake skidded, throwing gravel in all directions. Then it shot up in the air again, passing right over a small tree, and returned to a hill top close by.'

Michael had been sent out by his father, the owner of a vast farm in Keetmanshoop, to dispel the native mumbo-jumbo that had been costing him men and money. All of his farm workers had left after he ignored their stories of a giant flying snake that laired in the mountains where his sheep grazed. He finally deputised his boy to show the ignorant savages the folly of such beliefs. The boy did not return. He was later found unconscious and when he came to, related his dramatic tale. Oddly he related that the snake smelt of 'burned brass'. Police and farmer investigated in time to see the winged serpent crawl back into its cave. Lighted sticks of dynamite were hurled in after it. After the explosions they heard a low moaning for a while that gradually died away.

This incident was investigated by no less an authority than Dr Marjorie Courtenay-Latimer, a woman forever immortalised in the annals of cryptozoology as the discoverer of the coelacanth (*Latimeria chalumnae*), an archaic fish believed extinct for 65 million years. She interviewed the boy who took her to the spot of the attack. She did not see the beast but observed the great furrow it had made in the dust. She also noticed the lack of small animals such as birds and rats.

In 1988 Professor Roy Mackal, better known for his Congo excursions, investigated fantastic claims on a remote property owned by German settlers. Locals described a massive featherless creature with a nine metre wingspan that glided between two hills nearly two kilometres apart at dusk. The thing seemed to have lairs in crevices in the hills. Team members discovered the remains of ostrich carcasses in highly inaccessible areas and believed that the creatures had preyed on them, taking their kills back to the nest area. Mackal returned to the USA without having spied the animal but shortly afterwards one of his team members got lucky. James Kosi, who had stayed on in Namibia for a while saw the monster from a distance of around 300 metres. He described it as a giant glider, black with white markings.

In 1745 the book *The Harleian Collection of Travels* quoted Mr E. Lopes, a Portuguese man who travelled in the province of Bemba on the seacoast near the river Ambrize:

> 'There are also certain other creatures which, being as
> big as rams, have wings like dragons, with long tails,
> and long chaps, and divers rows of teeth, and feed
> upon raw flesh. Their colour is blue and green, their
> skin painted like scales, and they have two feet but
> no more. The pagan negroes used to worship them as
> gods, and at this day you may see divers of them that
> are kept as a marvel. And because they are very rare,
> the chief lords there curiously preserve them, and
> suffer the people to worship them, which tendeth

greatly to their profits by reason of the gifts and
obligations which the people offer unto them.'

John Barbot, Agent-General of the Royal Company of Africa spoke
of winged monsters inhabiting the coasts of South Guinea in the
1749 book *Collection of Voyages*:

> 'Some blacks assuring me that they [i.e. snakes] were
> thirty feet long. They also told me there are winged
> serpents or dragons having a forked tail and
> prodigious wide mouth, full of sharp teeth, extremely
> mischievous to mankind, and more particularly to
> small children. If we may credit this account of the
> blacks, they are the same sort of winged serpents
> which some authors tell us are to be found in
> Abyssinia, being great enemies to elephants. Some
> such serpents have been seen around the river
> Senegal, and they are adorned and worshiped as
> snakes are at Wida or Fida, that is, in a most religious
> manner.'

South and Central America

Quetzalcoatl was a god worshipped by the Aztecs. He took the form
of a giant winged serpent with feathers rather than scales. He was a
benevolent god who brought reading, books and cultivation to
mankind. By bringing back human bones from the underworld and
sprinkling them with his own blood he created the Aztec race. He
did not demand human sacrifice. He was eventually banished by his
evil twin Tezcatlipoca, god of the smoking mirror. Tezcatlipoca did
demand human sacrifice and it is said that one of the reasons the
Aztecs were defeated by the Conquistadors was that they hacked out
the hearts of 500 of their finest warriors in a sacrifice to him.

Quetzalcoatl sailed away on a raft of serpents. The Aztecs
supposedly mistook Cortez for the returning serpent god.
Quetzalcoatl could manifest as a white bearded man or a youth
with feathers in his hair.

The evil Tezcatlipoca had not always been at odds with his brother.
Once they teamed up to catch a gigantic dragon called Cipactil who
was half-crocodile and half-fish. Tezcatlipoca, presumably in human
form, acted as bait and lost his foot in the process. Together they
changed Cipactil into the land.

Further south in the Amazonian jungles we find dragon-like, rain-bringing powers attributed to the anaconda. The Marquis de Wavrin explored South America before the Second World War. He told the great Belgian cryptozoologist Bernard Heuvelmans that he had seen anacondas nearly ten metres long and the natives told of far larger ones. He once shot an eight metre individual that had been coiled around a branch. When he expressed a desire to retrieve the cadaver his canoe men told him that it was a waste of powder to shoot such a small snake and a waste of time picking it up. They went on to say:

> 'On the Rio Guaviare, during floods, chiefly in certain
> lagoons in the neighbourhood, and even near the
> confluence of this stream, we often see snakes that are
> more than double the size of the one you have just
> shot. They are often thicker than our canoe.'

Once, when Rio Uva was in flood, some Piapoco Indians tried to take a shortcut to the Rio Guaviare via some marshes and lagoons. Having just crossed a small lake the Indians heard a sound akin to thunder behind them, even though the rains had ceased and the skies were clear. Looking back the saw the waters in turmoil as a massive animal thrashed about in mid-water. Then a gigantic snake's head broke the surface and the animal disported itself momentarily before diving again. (Note here the interesting parallels with oriental dragons and their association with rain and storms.) The Indians believed that had the monster surfaced while they were crossing they would have been devoured. Not unreasonably they vowed never to take that particular shortcut again.

The Marquis himself only narrowly missed seeing a *sucuriju gigante*. He reached the Rio Putumayo the day after a giant boa had dragged off an ox. The people were still in a state of shock. He writes of these giants:

> 'Around the upper Paraguay they give the name
> *minocao* to a more or less fabulous snake: the natives
> say it can reach the size of a canoe. They suppose
> that it is a *sucuriju* or a boa-constrictor that has grown
> very old and turned into a water snake. On the upper
> Rio Parana, in Brazilian territory, I have also been told
> of these enormous snakes, capable of dragging a
> canoe to the bottom. These monsters frequent deserted
> places, and never leave a river. The fear they arouse
> is quite superstitious.'

Details of the Marquis and his adventures can be found in his 1951 book *Les Betes Sauvages de l' Amazonie.*

This idea of a giant serpent growing from as small snake is also seen in Asian dragon legends. The concept of a snake becoming too large to live on land and hence taking up an aquatic lifestyle echoes the Scandinavian lindorm stories.

Stories of encounters with giant anacondas are numerous and still reported today.

Another latter day basilisk is reported from the Caribbean. The eminent Victorian naturalist Phillip H. Gosse records it in *The Romance of Natural History, Second Series.* In 1845–6 Gosse visited Jamaica where he first heard of the creature from a respected medical man.

> '... he had seen, in 1829, a serpent about four feet in
> length, but of unwonted thickness, dull ochry in
> colour with well-defined dark spots, having on its
> head a sort of pyramidal helmet, somewhat lobed at
> the summit, of a pale red hue. The animal, however,
> was dead, and decomposition was already setting in.
> He informed me that the negroes of the district were
> well acquainted with it; and that they represented it as
> making a noise, not unlike the crowing of a cock, and
> being addicted to preying on poultry.'

Gosse's friend Richard Hill had heard of the snake from a Spanish acquaintance on Hispaniola. It was said to inhabit the eastern regions of the island.

> 'My friend's Spanish informant had seen the serpent
> with mandibles like a bird, with a cock's crest, with
> scarlet lobes or wattles; and he described its habits –
> perhaps from common fame rather than personal
> observation – as a frequenter of hen-roosts, into which
> it would thrust its head, and deceive the young
> chickens by its imitative physiognomy, and its
> attempts to crow.'

Jamaican resident Jasper Cargill offered a sovereign for any specimen of the snake but was not successful in obtaining one. Cargill himself had seen the illusive snake some years before as Gosse records.

> '... when visiting Skibo, in St George, an estate of his
> father's, in descending the mountain-road, his

attention was drawn to a snake of dark hue, that erected itself from some fragments of limestone rock that lay about. It was about four feet long and unusually thick bodied. His surprise was greatly increased on perceiving that it was crested, and that from the far side of its cheeks depended some red coloured flaps, like gills or wattles. After gazing at him intently for some time, with its head well erect, it drew itself in, and disappeared among the fragmentary rocks.'

Cargilll's son shot a specimen some years later.

'... some youngsters of the town came running to tell me of a curious snake, unlike any snake they had ever seen before, which young Cargill had shot, when out for a day's sport in the woodlands of a neighbouring penn. They described it as a serpent in all respects, but with a very curious shaped head, with wattles on each side of its jaws. After taking it in hand and looking at it, they placed it in a hollow tree, intending to return for it when they should be coming home, but they had strolled from the place so far that it was inconvenient to retrace their steps when wearied with rambling.'

When the youths returned the next day the corpse was missing, presumably taken by some scavenger. When the tale was recounted to Richard Hill his godson, Ulick Ramsay told him that he too had seen such a snake shortly before.

'... not long previously, he had seen in the hand of the barrack-master-sergeant at the barracks of a Spanish town, a curious snake, which he, too, had shot among the rocks of a little line of eminencies near the railway, about two miles out, called Craigallechie. It was a serpent with a curious shaped head, and projections on each side, which he likened to the fins of a eel, but said were close up to the jaws.'

North America

Many Indian tribes have legends of monstrous serpents. Most dwell in deep lakes or the ocean. The most famous legend is at Lake

Okanagan, in British Columbia, Canada. Legend holds that in the time of the Chinook Indians an old wise man lived by the lake. His name was Old Kan-He-Kan. The sage could communicate with animals and was a councillor for his people. One day an evil man called Kel-Oin-Won murdered the wise man. The distraught people named the lake Okanagan in his memory and the gods transformed his murderer into a gigantic serpent dragon, a creature so horrific that only rattlesnakes could tolerate his company. The beast was known as 'N'ha-a-itk'.

The Indians had a great fear of the dragon and believed that it could only be placated by sacrifice. If crossing the lake they would carry a chicken or some other small animal. These they tossed into the water for the monster to eat. One story tells of a visiting chief called Timbasket who ignored the advice of the local tribes. Both he and his canoe were never seen again.

The first non-native to clearly see Ogopogo was Susan Alison in 1872. She was looking across the lake for her husband, who was due to return from a trip. She saw a strange animal swimming against the waves. She had studied native folklore and realised that this must be the dreaded N'ha-a-itk. She was filled with foreboding that the creature had destroyed her husband's vessel and eaten him. Upon her husband's return she told him of her sighting but was not believed. She wrote an atmospheric little poem about her sighting:

> Miles to westward lies an island
> An island all men dread,
> A rocky barren island,
> Where a monster makes his bed.
> So busy are the fishers
> That they hardly spare a glance
> To the black line of white crested waves,
> That so rapidly advance.
> From the westward from the island,
> The island all men dread,
> From the rocky barren island,
> Where the monster makes his bed.

The island in question is Rattlesnake Island off Squally Point. Mrs Alison's husband may have laughed but soon others had seen the serpent. John McDouall, for example, would certainly not laugh. He was a trader who always crossed the lake by canoe with his horses in tow. On one occasion in 1860 he was horrified to see his horses dragged one by one beneath the surface. He had to cut the towrope to prevent his canoe being pulled under.

Early settlers took the threat of N`ha-a-itk very seriously and carried guns whenever they were close to lake. In 1926 a ferry operating on the lake was armed in case of attack by the monster.

It was also in 1926 that the monster got its modern name 'Ogopogo'. The name comes from an English music hall ballad of 1924 written by Cumberland Clark and sung by Mark Strong. It concerns the hunt for a banjo-playing monster called 'Ogopogo' in the hills of Hindustan and runs:

> I'm looking for the Ogopogo,
> The funny little Ogopogo.
> His mother was an earwig,
> His father was a whale.
> I'm going to put a little bit of salt on his tail.
> I want to find the Ogopogo
> While he's playing on his old Banjo.
> The Lord Mayor of London
> Wants to put him in the Lord Mayor's show.

Quite why the name was applied to the Okanagan monster is anyone's guess but it stuck and the lake monster has become far better known around the world than the almost forgotten music hall song.

The dragon has been spotted hundreds of times. Typical is the report by Mrs E.A. Campbell who was sitting with two friends on the lawn of her home on the afternoon of 6th July 1952 when they saw Ogopogo a few hundred feet out on the lake. Mrs Campbell said:

> 'I am a stranger here. I did not even know such things
> existed. But I saw it so plainly. A head like a cow or
> a horse that reared right up out of the water. It was a
> wonderful sight. The coils glistened like two huge
> wheels going around and around. The edges were all
> ragged like that of a saw. It was so beautiful with the
> sun shining on it. It was all so very clear, so
> extraordinary, as it came up three times, submerged
> and disappeared.'

Many other lakes across North America have their own dragon traditions. Canada lays claim to having more lake monsters than any other country in the world. But these creatures are not only reported from fresh water. The Indians of the western Canadian coast have long known of sea dragons in the area and recorded them in rock art and carvings. The Chinook of British Columbia called it 'hiachuckaluck'. The Hurons of Saint Lawrence Valley knew it as 'angoub'. To the Manhousat of Flores Island and the Sydney Inlet it was 'hiyitl`iik'.

F.W. Kemp, an officer of the Provisional Archives gave the most detailed account. He made his report to the *Victoria Daily Times* in 1933:

> 'On Aug 10, 1932, I was with my wife on Chatham Island in the Strait of Jaun de Fuca. My wife called my attention to a mysterious something coming through the channel between Strong Tide Island and Chatham Island. Imagine my astonishment on observing a huge creature with head out of the water travelling about four miles per hour against the tide. Even at that speed a considerable wash was thrown against the rocks, that gave the impression that it was more reptile [i.e. lizard or saurian] than serpent to make so much displacement.
>
> The channel at this point is about 500 yards wide. Swimming to the steep rocks of the island opposite, the creature shot its head out of the water on to the rock, and moving its head from side to side, appeared to be taking its bearings. Then fold after fold if its body came to the surface. Towards the tail it appeared serrated with something moving flail like at the extreme end. The movements were like those of a crocodile. Around the head appeared a sort of mane, which drifted round the body like kelp.
>
> The thing's presence seemed to change the whole landscape, which makes it difficult to describe my experiences. It did not seem to belong to the present scheme of things, but rather to the Long Ago when the world was young. The position it held on the rocks was momentary. My wife and sixteen year old son ran to a point of land to get a better view. I think the sound they made disturbed the animal. The sea being very calm, it seemed to slip back into deep water; there was a great

97

commotion under the surface and it disappeared like a flash.

In my opinion its speed must be terrific and its senses of smell, sight, and hearing developed to a very high degree. It would be terribly hard to photograph, as its movements are different from anything I have ever seen or heard of. I say its length to be not less than 80 ft. There were some logs on Strong Tide Island which gave me a good idea of the size of the monster as it passed them. I took a measurement of one the next day which was over 60 ft, and the creature overlapped it to a large extent at each end. I put a newspaper on the spot it rested and took an observation from our previous point of vantage. The animal's head was very much larger than the double sheet of newspaper. The body must have been at least five feet thick, and was of a bluish-green colour, which shone in the sun like aluminium. I could not determine the shape of the head, but it was much thicker than the body.'

The beast, christened 'Caddy', has been reported by white settlers from the mid-1800s right up to the present day.

The creatures may well come further south as sea dragons have been reported in the warmer waters of the seaboard of the western USA.

Such a dragon first reared its head in 1976 near San Francisco. The Great Western Pacific Report ran a story about Tom D`Onofrio, a minister from Bolinas. Tom`s account runs:

'On September 30, 1976, at 12 noon I experienced the most overwhelming event in my life. I was working on a carved dragon to use as a base for a table and couldn't complete the head. I felt compelled to go down to Agate Beach were I met a friend, Dick Borgstrom.

Suddenly, 150 feet from shore, gambolling in an incoming wave, was this huge dragon, possibly 60 feet long and 15 feet wide.

The serpent seemed to be playing in the waves, threshing its tail. We were so overpowered by the sight we were rooted to the spot for about 10 minutes. I literally felt as if I were in the presence of God. My life has changed since.'

A colourful account, and one that would have probably attracted little attention if the monster had not returned. Upon its second visit the dragon was seen by an entire road construction crew from the Californian Department of Transportation. On 1st November 1983 they were on a cliff top road, Highway 1, just south of Stinson Beach. It was 2.30 in the afternoon. Safety engineer Marlene Martin takes up the story:

> 'The flagman at the north end of the job-site hollered, 'What's that in the water?'
>
> We all looked out to sea but could see nothing so the flagman, Matt Ratto, got his binoculars. Finally I saw the wake and I said, 'Oh my God, its coming right at us, real fast.'
>
> There was a large wake on the surface and the creature was submerged about a foot under the water. At the base of the cliff it lay motionless for about five seconds and we could look directly down and see it stretched out. I decided it must have been 100 feet long, and like a big black hose about five feet in diameter. I didn't see the end of the tail.
>
> It then made a U-turn and raced back, like a torpedo, out to sea. All of a sudden, it thrust its head out of the water, its mouth went towards the sky, and it thrashed about.
>
> Then it stopped, coiled itself up into three humps of the body and started to whip about like an uncontrolled hosepipe. It did not swim sideways like a snake, but up and down.
>
> I had binoculars and kept them focused on the head. It had the appearance of a snake-like dinosaur; making coils and throwing its head about, splashing and opening its mouth. The teeth were peg like and even – there were no fangs. The head resembled the way people drew dragons except it wasn't so long. It looked gigantic and ferocious.

I did not see any fins or flippers and it had bothered me that it could move so fast in that way. It was scientifically impossible for anything to go that fast without them. It was not like a snake going sideways, it went up and down.

It stunned me, never in my life could I ever have imagined a thing so huge could go so fast. I thought, when I saw it, this is a myth.

I've never really told anybody this before and I cannot swear to it but the eye I saw looked like it was red, a deep burgundy-ruby colour. When I think about the thing I still see that colour and what's amazing about it is that I've never seen that particular red on anything before.'

The most detailed account of the monster was given by Bill and Bob Clark who saw it on 5th February 1985:

'From the start this particular morning was different. The day before had been beautiful with no wind and temperatures of 70 degrees. The fifth was just gorgeous, with a clear sky, calm water, and high tide. We had never seen the San Francisco Bay so calm. It was like looking in a mirror. Anything sticking above the surface of the water was easily seen. As a result, at around 7.45 a.m., we noticed a group of sea lion about 150 yards in front of us. While watching them, we thought we saw another sea lion come around Stone Tower point and approach the group. When it got within a few yards a long, black, tubular object telescoped about ten feet straight out of the water and lunged forward almost falling on top of the sea lions. They immediately began swimming away, leaping in and out of the water as the fled toward shore.

The creature churned the water as it swam behind them moving so fast it was a blur, but we could see three or four vertical undulations moving down the length of the animal. Suddenly, it went underwater. Meanwhile the sea lions were coming closer and closer to where we were parked along the Marina Green only yards from the bay. They came so close that Bob was able to make eye contact with one and see the fear of death in its eyes as it leaped out of the water. The creature followed close behind string up the water as it made a final attempt to procure a meal.

Now only 25 yards away, an arch of the animal was exposed, which looked like half a truck tier. It appeared black and slimy, yet at the same time glistened in the early sunlight. The creature was swimming slightly below the surface almost parallel to the shore. The water was very clear allowing the outline of the serpent's head to be observable. A short flat snout, eyebrow ridges, and lots of neck could be seen. It must have been 30 feet of neck because we both thought a big snake had just swam by. We were expecting to see the end of the snake but instead of getting smaller it began to get much larger. What we watched wasn't a big snake but something even more unbelievable.

There was a loud crash and with a spray of water the creature seemed to stop dead in its tracks (later at low tide the next day we realised that a ledge with large rocks on it extended 20 yards into the bay at the location where the creature crashed). Instantaneously, a long black neck popped up, twisting backwards away from the shore, then splashed as it hit the surface of the water and disappeared. The serpent twisted clockwise like a corkscrew and exposed its midsection above the water, giving us an excellent view of the underbelly, which was creamy white with a tint of yellow. It resembled an alligator's belly with a soft leathery look but was divided into many sections several feet wide. The midsection was about 20 feet long, black on top, and slowly changed from a mossy green to a grassy green and ultimately to a yellow-green as it approached the underbelly. It had hexagonal scales next to each other rather than overlapping. The largest scales appeared at the widest part of the midsection where the underbelly and the side of the creature met, gradually reducing in size as they approached the top, front and end of the midsection. The largest scales were bigger than a silver dollar and the smallest were the size of a dime. There was a distinct line were the texture of the skin changed from scales to the smooth, leathery underbelly.

While it continued twisting, another section six to nine feet long arched upwards three feet above the water. The arch twisted away from us exposing a fan-like appendage that was attached to its side at the waterline. It looked like a flag flapping in the wind. It was triangular in shape with a serrated outer edge. Mossy green ribbing ran from a single point attached to the side of the animal like the spokes of a wheel. A paper-thin green membrane stretched between each rib which extended farther than the membrane, creating a serrated edge. The appendage was equilateral with each side almost two feet in length reminding us of a 'dragon's wing'. Bob concentrated on counting the ribs but stopped when he got to six as there were too many. Bill looked at the rest of the animal and saw two appendages, one at the beginning and one at the end of the midsection. They looked like stabilizer fins as opposed to flippers for propulsion. Slowly the body sank beneath the water onto the rocks below. Under the surface of the water we could see the upper section of the neck. Four tightly folded coils were formed directly behind the head.

The creature moved its neck with a whipping motion and the four coils travelled backwards in a packet, dissipating upon reaching the midsection. Instantly it created another packet of four coils behind the head and again these were whipped backwards toward the midsection. This was repeated several times until the creature began to pull itself into deeper water. It was like watching a freight train pull out of a station, each section had to wait for the section in front to move.

The outline of the head could be seen as it sat underwater but no details were observable except a snake-like head with large jowls. When it began to swim north toward the middle of the bay we thought we saw a ridgeline along the top of the rear section. However, we never saw the tail. As it swam away at a leisurely pace, several arches could be seen undulating above the water. A few seconds later it sloped beneath the water. Since we never saw the rear end of the animal it is hard to estimate the total length but it had to be at least sixty feet and probably closer to a hundred feet.'

The Clark twins saw the creature several more times in the next few years.

The whaling grounds of New England on America's east coast were once home to a similar sea dragon. In the summer of 1817 off Cape Ann near Gloucester, Massachusetts a whole wave of sightings occurred. On 6th August two women saw one enter the harbour at Cape Ann. Most people ignored their story but it was seen again by a number of fishermen. Amos Story, a seaman, saw it near Ten Pound Island. On 10th August Solomon Allen, a shipmaster, saw it from a boat. On the 14th thirty people, including the Hon. Lonson Nash, Justice of the Peace for Gloucester. Mathew Gaffney, a ship's carpenter, fired a musket ball at its head from point blank range. The monster was not in the slightest affected.

From then on the creatures visited the area every year until the 1840s when the sightings dropped off sharply. This may have been a result of human disturbance.

Australasia

The Aboriginal tribes of Australia have many legends of dragon-like monsters.

Mungoon galli, the goanna bunyip, whipped up sand storms with his mighty tail in much the same way as the Chinese believed dragons controlled the weather. This is one of the many 'coincidences' to be found when one studies dragon lore worldwide.

Mungoon galli may have been based on a very real animal.

One of the most spectacular reptilian macro-predator must have been the giant varanid or monitor lizard *Megalania prisca*. This immense lizard reached lengths of ten metres, rivalling the largest contemporary crocodiles. Much like a scaled-up Komodo Dragon, *Megalania* preyed on the large herbivores of its time although its sheer size and power suggests it probably relied less on viral killing. The Aborigines arrived at least 40,000 years ago. Sharing their environment with such a monster (almost certainly a man-eater) was daunting indeed and *Megalania* etched itself onto the Aboriginal culture.

Most believe that *Megalania* died out at least 10,000 years ago but there is a chance that it or something closely-related still stalks the outback.

The Aborigines have always told of encountering giant lizards but as Australia began to be colonised by white men they too crossed paths with the lord of the outback. One of the first sightings took place in 1890 at the village of Euroa, Victoria. A ten metre lizard came lumbering out of the bush causing panic and leaving a trail of king-sized footprints. A posse of forty men armed with guns and nets set out with cattle dogs to trap the monster. The beast had other ideas and vanished into the scrub to be seen no more.

Three loggers reported a giant lizard in May 1961. They were in a remote part of the Wauchop forest in New South Wales. Having marked some trees for felling the trio sat down to brew tea in a previously cleared area. This place was now covered in rotting wood and the loggers heard the crunching of something large approaching them. Looking up they saw a titanic lizard bearing down on them from an embankment. Fleeing in terror the three locked themselves in their truck and watched horrified as the dragon stalked across the dirt track and back into the forest. All agreed its length was ten metres and held its body a metre off the ground.

Perhaps the most important sighting happened in 1979 in the Wattagan mountains, also in New South Wales, as it involved a professional herpetologist, a scientist who specialises in the study of reptiles. Frank Gorden had taken his four-wheel drive Land Rover into the mountains to look for tiny lizards known as water skinks. After several unfruitful hours searching Gorden returned to his vehicle and noticed a large 'log' lying on a two metre-high bank next to the land rover. Gorden could not recall this log being there before but thought nothing of it until he turned the ignition causing the 'log' to rear up on four powerful legs and charge off into the woods. Gorden, who was left in a mild state of shock, estimated it to be 28 to 30 feet long (about 9 metres) in comparison to his Land Rover. It is highly appropriate that after failing to find any tiny lizards he found one very big one! When a recognised expert in the field sees an animal like this, close up and with a frame of reference for size doubts about its existence are seriously eroded.

The above is just a sampler of these stories. I have many, many more reports of giant lizard sightings in Australia on file.

There is a lot of archaeological evidence that suggests the ancient Chinese reached Australia centuries before Captain Cook. These include artefacts unearthed in Australia and ancient Chinese maps that seem to show the great island continent.

In 338 BC Chinese scholar Shin Tzu wrote of animals kept at the Imperial zoo in Peking. One description is that of a kangaroo, obviously this must have come from Australia either directly or via trade in the south Pacific.

It is tempting to theorise that these Chinese mariners met with the great Australia lizard and it was one of the influences on oriental dragon lore.

Australia cannot claim monopoly on giant lizards, as its close neighbour New Guinea also has its own dragons. In the Second World War Japanese soldiers caught glimpses of what they described as 'tree climbing crocodiles' deep in the Papuan jungle. Then in the summer of 1960 the *News Chronicle* reported that a panic had broken out on the island as rumours that people had been killed by six or seven metre long dragons began to circulate. The monsters were said to breathe fire and drink blood. Their victims were left with thirty centimetre-long claw marks in the flesh. The scare became so bad that the government authorities moved people into stockades and offered substantial rewards for the capture of one of the beasts. The reward went unclaimed, the dragons disappeared and the riddle went unsolved.

Robert Grant and David George were exploring the Strachan Island district in 1961 when they encountered a grey skinned lizard some 8 metres long. The creature's neck alone measured one metre.

In the mid-1980s famed British explorer Colonel John Blashford-Snell was told of the 'tree climbing crocodile'. Locals called it 'Artrellia' and seemed to go in great fear of it. Blashford-Snell was told that it stands upright and breaths fire. From the descriptions of an old chief he sketched an animal looking much like a dinosaur. One story told of a young warrior many years ago, who was hunting deep in the forest. Feeling weary he sat down on a log. The 'log' in now familiar style revealed itself as a dragon. It towered three metres tall on its hind legs and possessed toothy crocodile-like jaws. The man fled back to his village in terror.

Intrigued, the colonel hit the trail. No less a man than the brother of the Premier of the Western Province told him that an elderly man had died in the Daru hospital after being attacked by a female Artrellia protecting her nest. A village elder also said the creatures could grow to over three metres long and often stood on their hind legs, lending them a dinosaur-like appearance. They were arboreal and leapt down onto their prey that they killed with their huge claws and infectious bite. Even small specimens were feared; recently a small one had been captured and placed in a wooden cage. It swiftly broke free and killed a large dog before escaping back into the jungle.

In 1999 two groups of people spotted a dinosaur-like creature at Lake Murry near Boroko. It was six metres long with crocodile-like skin. It had thick hind legs with smaller front limbs and a long tail.

Winged dragons are reported from this area as well. The Duah is said to be a flying reptile with a six metre wingspan and a crested head. In 1995 villagers from Gum-along reported seeing a Duah swoop down from Mount Bel, soar over a jungle valley and then head out to sea. The monster's underbelly was allegedly bioluminescent and glowed.

The Duah has a smaller relative on the island of Rambunzu off Papua New Guinea's east coast. It is known as the 'Ropen' and has a wingspan of just over a metre. It trails a long tail terminating in a diamond-shaped fin. The Ropen is allegedly an aggressive beast like its African counterparts. It is attracted by the smell of decaying flesh and is said to attack funeral gatherings. Western missionaries have observed this and attacks on fishing boats where the Ropen has snatched fish from the nets. These mini-dragons are believed to roost in caves like bats.

Stories of giant winged monsters in New Guinea are nothing new. On page 76 of *Nature* volume 13 published in November 1875 there is an account of an encounter with such a beast. A Mr Smithurst, an engineer on a steamer that travelled up the recently discovered Baxter River, saw a gigantic 'bird'. It was brown, with a white breast, long neck and straight beak. The wingspan was five to six metres. Natives told him that it could carry off turtles, kangaroos and dugongs.

These legends and their counterparts in latter-day sightings are just the tip of the iceberg. Of all the 'mythical' beasts, dragons are most often reported in the modern age.

Chapter Six
What are dragons?

Religious and cultural influence

In times of great social upheaval or unrest people report strange things. It is a well-attested phenomenon. Perhaps some dragon legends are a metaphor for such distressing or confusing times. The dominant religious or social power may also wish to demonise its rivals or past contenders making them into monsters. Remember history is written by the winning side so an invading force or disruptive element may be recalled as a monster.

When the Romans invaded Britain they brought with them dragon standards. These were a kind of monstrous windsock. They consisted of a metallic head attached to a pole held by the bearer. Fastened to the head was a long cloth body. The wind billowed through the cloth causing it to inflate and writhe. The metal teeth made a hissing sound striking fear into the foe. These standards were used by cohorts (one tenth of a legion) and indeed the Latin for a standard bearer is *draconarius*. Perhaps the stories of an oppressive and powerful force sweeping into the country under the dragon standard evolved into the story a serpentine creature bringing a reign of terror.

The greatest of all warrior races were the Vikings. Their berserker furies were the stuff of legend. When in this altered state of battle madness they were imbued with terrifying strength and savagery making them peerless in battle. Perhaps the carved dragon heads of their long ships metamorphosed into literal dragons in the retelling of their raids. Their influence was particularly felt in the north-east of England that eventually fell under their rule. The dragon's infamous greed and hoarding of treasure may have had its genesis in the booty the Norse men carried away from towns, castles and monasteries. The Danegeld demanded by the Vikings is akin to the people in worm legends trying to pacify the monster with offerings of livestock and milk. A dragon-headed, elongated monster that emerges from the water to terrorise the population, kills all who oppose it and take what it wants is a good metaphor for oppression by the Vikings.

Another Viking/dragon link is the old Norse tradition that dead men can be transformed into treasure-guarding dragons. This occurs in many Sagas including the *Gull-Thoris Saga, Egils Saga Skallagrimssonar, Bardar Saga, Halfdanar Saga, Eysteinssonar* and *Porskfiroinga Saga.* The best-known example is that of Fafnir who becomes a dragon after years of sitting on a horde of gold in Wagner's *Siegfried.*

The idea of spontaneous generation may seem odd to us but it has a very old pedigree. In Greece and Rome it was thought that human spinal cords became serpents after death. In Norton Fitzwarren a dragon was supposedly generated from masses of human corpses.

In the early eleventh century Byrhtferth, a monk at Ramsey Abbey wrote: 'What are dragons but depraved men and ones keen for conflict and the enemies of God and their own soul's destruction?' This sounds like a description of Viking raiders.

The idea of a dragon slayer might be metaphor for Christianity chasing out other, older religions. Christianity is a patriarchal religion with a solar hero (Christ). We should note with interest that in AD 274 the Emperor Aurelian instigated December 25th as the holy day of the new state religion that had the Sun as its chief deity. One solar hero replaced another. The solar hero is a recurring motif in legend. He usually defeats a dragon or serpent that holds back cosmic waters or hides the rays of the sun. The eternal battle between Ra and Apophis is one example, Marduk and Tiamat in Mesopotamia is another. St Michael as a solar hero hardly needs introducing.

We know little about the origins of the Church in Britain. The first Christians in Britain were probably some of the Roman soldiers based here in the first century AD. The first Christian emperor of Rome was Constantine (AD 280–337) who is said to have become a Christian after dreaming of Jesus the night before a battle. He is also famed for moving the capital of the Roman Empire to Constantinople (now Istanbul) in Turkey. Here we may find the key to the link between dragons and paganism.

In Turkey a serpent worship cult flourished. It was said to have its roots in Ur. The priests supposedly fled the Persians and came to Pergamos in Lydia (western Turkey). They were supposed to have brought the physical manifestation of their god with them. The beast they worshipped is shown on a carving in Pompeii and has a horned serpentine head and humped body. The same thing decorates an Urarian cauldron, depicted with an erect head and neck and a large mouth. The serpent god looks like nothing known to science but does recall descriptions of lake and sea monsters.

The serpent cult seems to have caught on in Rome according to Seneca in his *Historia August*. He states that snakes known as *dracunculi* were kept in Roman houses. These were probably the harmless Aesculapian snake *(Elaphe longissima)* that the Greeks had associated with Asclepius. But something far larger was supposedly brought to Rome.

When the Roman Empire annexed Turkey in AD 133, after the death of Attalus III (last of the Pergamite kings), a plague had broken out in Rome and a special ship was dispatched to carry the Turkish serpent god from Lydia to Rome where the deity was installed. The plague may have run its course naturally but it coincided with the strange cargo from Turkey. The improvement in health would have been attributed to the serpent god.

Worship of such creatures persisted well into the times of Christian Rome. Tertullian complained that: 'These heretics magnify the serpent to such a degree as to prefer him even to Christ himself.' If these strange stories were true then Constantine would have likened paganism to serpents and dragons. Flushing out of these cults may have transformed over time into dragon legends.

Mention is made of the Church in Britain from Tertullian, an African who wrote at the end of the second century, but the information is scant. There is a tradition that some British Christians were put to death for their faith about 100 years later – St Alban was the best known. The British Church first appears in the records of history in the year 314, when three bishops from this country were present at a council held at Arles in the south of France. British bishops from the same era were present at other religious councils, showing that they were in communion with the rest of the Church in the Empire. In the early fifth century there is evidence that the Church in Britain was expanding. But then Rome itself began to crumble. Later the Anglo-Saxons conquered Britain and paganism rose again. Not until the Roman monk Augustine landed in Kent nearly 150 years later, in 597, did the conversion of the pagan Anglo-Saxons begin. Here may be a second 'chasing out of the dragon'.

In his book *The Myths of Reality* Simon Danser gives us a plausible reason why dragons are associated with underground caverns.

> '... 'up/down' is an especially rich and complex metaphor in western thinking. We see the future as 'up' ('What's coming up this week?'). 'Up' is unknown ('The decision's still up in the air') and down is 'settled'. We 'wake up' and 'fall asleep'. More is up ('My pay went up') and less is down ('Sales have gone down'). Virtue is up ('She has high standards') and depravity is down ('Doing that's beneath me'). Status is high or low ('He's well up the corporate ladder'; 'They are near the bottom of the social hierarchy'). Spirituality is up ('heavenly', 'angelic') and the mundane world is 'down to earth' or – on a bad day – 'hellish', with its implications of the Underworld.
>
> 'The up/down metaphor extrapolates into mythical concepts. Below the everyday world is a mythical 'other world' of fairies living in hollow hills, dragons living in underground lairs, the fires of Hell, and such like. Nothing changes much in modern day thinking – we continue to demonise the 'underworld', linking it metaphorically with criminals.'

Shapes in the landscape

In many dragon legends the monster leaves some kind of mark upon the landscape. Here we could evoke the chicken and egg question. Which came first? Were some dragon legends created to explain odd bits of topography?

The best-known example is the rings around Penshaw Hill where the Lambton worm is said to have coiled itself and left squeeze marks in the very earth. In fact Penshaw Hill was once an Iron Age fort and the 'coils' are the ramparts.

A worm was also said to have coiled about Bignor Hill in Sussex leaving its marks. These have an even more prosaic explanation. They are pathways worn by sheep following the hill's contours.

At Anwick in Lincolnshire there is a huge boulder that a dragon is said to have emerged from under. At Walmsgate in Lincolnshire a dragon is said to be buried in a long barrow. The lack of grass on Dragon Hill, Berkshire is a supposed consequence of the ground

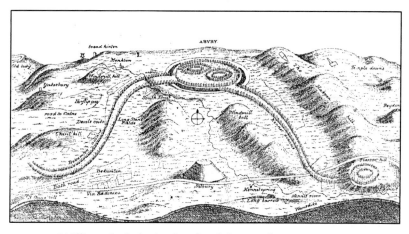

William Stukeley's sketch of the Avebury 'serpents'.

being burnt by dragon's blood. The dragon of the Exe Valley had two lairs in Iron Age forts. The list goes on.

Just because a certain facet of a legend is explained as in the coils about Penshaw and Bignor Hills, we should not throw out the baby with the bath water. Ancient storytellers may have elaborated to bring a local landmark into a story to make it more immediate and exciting as well as explaining an odd feature as being made by a dragon.

The idea of the land being sculpted by dragons is turned on its head by people landscaping the land to look like a dragon. Many believe that this has been done a number of times in Britain. The eighteenth century antiquarian William Stukeley believed that the impressive stone circle and avenues at Avebury, Wiltshire, depicted a serpent and showed evidence of a serpent worship cult in ancient Britain.

Stukeley thought that the Sanctuary (a modern name for concentric prehistoric timber circles of unknown purpose) atop Overton Hill to the south-east of the main monument was the serpent's head. This head was linked to the main monument (that he took to be the coiled body) by a winding avenue of paired standing stones. Another avenue once wound from the other side of the Avebury circle to a long barrow at Beckhampton. This he thought represented the serpent's tail. The whole monument could be viewed as a giant snake with its head and tail stretched out from the main body.

111

F.W. Holliday, author of *The Dragon and the Disc* alleges that a Bronze Age dragon cult built great images of their gods out of earth and stone. One is on the banks of the River Clyde and another in Ach na Goul near Inverary. A hundred metre dragon simulacra is at the lower end of Loch Nell. John S. Phene described it to the British Association in Edinburgh as being in the form of a serpent or saurian. A similar construction is to be found near in Glen Feochan near Oban. He wrote up his findings in a book *Serpent Worship in the West.*

According to Holliday the most spectacular example is on the ridge of Ben Cruachan above the Pass of Brander, overlooking Loch Awe. The three natural peaks have (according to both Holliday and Phene) been utilised to form the monster's humps while a manmade cairn is the head. Phene found a megalithic tomb under the head cairn, containing charcoal, charred nutshells, flint tools and burned bones. Perhaps it is no coincidence that these structures were erected close to deep bodies of water in Scotland.

Mazes may have been linked to serpent worship. Many ancient mazes were cut into turf on hilltops or hillsides. Some still exist, including one at Saffron Walden where a basilisk was alleged to have lived. The mazes are usually spiral and resemble serpent's coils. They may have been used in spiralling serpent dances now long-forgotten. We may gain some knowledge of what these serpent dances were like by looking at counterparts on mainland Europe. The *Schlangenweg* or 'serpent way' was a name used for turf labyrinths in Germanic countries. A serpent dance called *Schlanggenziehen* is held in the German town of Naumburg. The line of dancers snake around maypoles and linden trees to the sound of music. The image recalls the great serpent coiling about the Tree of Life. Indeed many mazes had trees at the centre. The Rad Ma at the Eilenriede Forest in Hanover, Germany still has a linden tree at its centre. An ash once stood at the centre of the maze on the common at basilisk haunted Saffron Walden. It was burnt down on Guy Fawkes' Night, 1823.

Meteorological phenomena

The *Anglo-Saxon Chronicles* are the closest thing in the Middle Ages to newspapers. They were begun on the orders of King Alfred the Great in around AD 890 and were kept in various places until the middle of the twelfth century, ending at around the same time as the reign of King Stephen drew to a close in 1154. The combined records run to over 100,000 words. The earlier entries are written in Old English and the later ones in Middle English. They were first properly translated by the Rev James Ingram in 1823.

The *Chronicles* records all manner of strange occurrences, often at the time they happened, and also back-references notable events as far as AD 1. There are a number of recorded sighting of dragons in the *Chronicles*:

> AD 497 A star of Marvellous size and brilliancy appeared, shining in one single ray, attached to which ray was a ball of fire in the shape of a dragon, and out of its mouth proceeded two rays.

> AD 793. This year came dreadful fore-warnings over the land of the Northumbrians, terrifying the people most woefully: these were immense sheets of light rushing through the air, and whirlwinds, and fiery, dragons flying across the firmament. These tremendous tokens were soon followed by a great famine.

> AD 795. Fearfull lightnings and dragons blazing in a dreadfull manner were seen to fly through the air, signs which forshadowed a mighty famine.

> AD 1066. A dragon was seen in the sky at the time when King Harold was Killed at the Battle of Hastings.

Other later documents also speak of dragons. In 1170, the seventh year of the reign of King Henry II, a dragon was seen in St Osythes, Essex and described as 'of marvellous bigness, which by moving, burned houses.' 1177 saw many dragons reported in the sky, a great wind, and an eclipse before Christmas. In 1221 dragons and spirits were seen flying during a violent storm. The same thing was reported over London the next year.

Two huge dragons were seen fighting in the sky off the southern coast of England in 1233. The victor chased the vanquished beneath the sea. This was followed by a time of strife between the King and his barons.

In 1274 during the vigil of St Nicholas there was an earthquake, thunder and lightning. A comet and a dragon appeared.

In 1395 a shape-shifting dragon seen in Nottinghamshire and Leicestershire. It was said to manifest in the shape of a spinning wheel of fire, a flaming barrel and a burning lace.

A whole flock of dragons numbering up to one hundred and sporting pig-like snouts were reported from all across Britain in 1532.

Some of these like the last report sound like some kind of living creature. But many of the others sound more like some kind of meteorological phenomenon filtered through the eyes of contemporary people who would not have properly understood it. Perhaps what was being referred to was a comet or meteor, such as Halley's comet in 1066.

The great dragon Typhon who battled the gods of ancient Greece has been identified as a comet. The Roman writer Pliny in his *Natural History* specifically identifies this cosmic dragon with comets.

> 'There was a dreadfull one (comet) observed by the
> Ethiopians and the Egyptians, to which Typhon, a king
> of that period, gave his own name; it had a fiery
> appearance, and twisted like a spiral; its aspect was
> hideous, nor was it like a star, but rather like a ball of
> fire.'

One can readily imagine what a stir a meteor burning up in the atmosphere, or a comet trailing, serpent-like across the primordial night sky, would have had in bygone years. In times past it seems that comets such as Halley's came much closer to the Earth than they have in the past couple of centuries. Such a spectacular sight could have thrown whole nations into a panic.

How much more terrible the fear if a meteor actually struck the earth? Most of us have heard of the Tunguska event. At 7.17 a.m. on 8th June 1908 something exploded above a remote area of Siberian forest with a force of 10 to 15 megatonnes. Contemporary reports speak of people seeing a ball of fire or a 'second sun'. The blast felled 60 million trees over an area of 2,150 square kilometres. People 650 kilometres away were knocked down by the shock wave and for several weeks subsequently the night sky was illuminated so much that one could read a newspaper by it.

The Tunguska event is believed to have been caused by a meteor 60 metres across. Until recently it was thought that objects such as these enter the Earth's atmosphere only rarely, perhaps every 300 years or so. But recent research has challenged this. Two meteors of a similar size to the Tunguska object seem to have fallen in South

America in the 1930s. They devastated huge areas of jungle but were too remote to explore. In the early 1950s a spectacular piece of film was shot of a glowing meteor trailing a tail of smoke and fire. The object was mistaken for a UFO and was not identified until experts saw the film. It was estimated that the meteor caught on camera was marginally smaller that the Tunguska object. Luckily it hit the Earth's atmosphere at such an angle that it skimmed like a pebble on water and was deflected. With just a few degrees difference in entry it would have torn through the atmosphere and smashed into the Canadian city of Calgary, killing millions. If such an object hit central London everything as far away as the Watford Gap service station in Northamptonshire would be destroyed.

More recently, in early 1999, something lit up the night sky over Europe. At 5.15 a.m. trawler men on three separate ships off southern Greenland reported a strange flash and odd lights in the sky. Surveillance cameras in northern Europe captured a weird flash. Seismographs in Finland, Denmark, Norway and Germany recorded a ten second shock. There were also reports of a vast cloud of steam.

The object struck a remote area 48 km north-east of Narsuruaq Airport near the settlement of Julianehab. Five billion tons of ice were vaporised. Once again, a slight change of angle would have brought this meteor down on Europe destroying cities or raising titanic waves hundreds of feet high that would have swept miles inland.

Yet more recently, what was believed to have been a meteor or a comet's nucleus smashed into a Siberian mountainside in 2002. The object struck at 10 p.m. on 25th September close to the town of Bodaybo in the Mamsko-Chuisky district of Irkustsk Oblast. An official expedition failed to reach the site but an aerial photograph shows a huge area blasted clean of vegetation.

That makes a total of six meteors of deadly size striking the earth within one century rather than one every three centuries. Even much smaller objects would cause awful destruction in localised areas and probably live in legend for centuries afterwards. Could such events in the past have given rise to tales of cosmic conflict between the gods and a primal chaos dragon? Did early people interpret meteors striking the Earth as the wrath of a dragon?

One man who believed comets and meteors were responsible for dragon legends was Immanuel Velikovsky. Velikovsky was a Jewish psychiatrist born in 1895. In 1940 he theorised that many of the world-shaking events in the Old Testament had been caused by natural disasters. He thought that some cosmic upheaval may have been the cause. Ten years later he published his most controversial book *Worlds In Collision.* Herein Velikovsky postulated that the solar system was a macrocosm of the atom. In an atom electrons revolving about the nucleus jump from one orbit to another when struck by the energy of a proton. On an unimaginably larger scale and longer time span, he contended, the solar system is the same. Planets move from orbit to orbit over thousands of years causing catastrophe on Earth.

For example, in the second millennium BC, he maintains, Venus (formerly part of Jupiter according to him) had come close to the Earth causing the Earth's axis to change and the polar regions to move. The meteors that showered the Earth at such times were remembered as dragons spitting down flames, as were long-tailed comets.

Velikovsky believed that all the great disasters in recorded history from the Babylonians onward had been caused by such planetary shifts. He also postulated a dragon cult beginning in Neolithic times, spreading worldwide and lasting for millennia. The cult practised human sacrifice to appease the cosmic serpent (or comet). Velikovsky and his theories have been roundly rebuffed by experts. We must recall that he was a psychiatrist not an astronomer, physicist or archaeologist. There is no evidence to support his planetary movement theories.

While Velikovsky was almost certainly wrong in the main thrust of his argument there may be some truths in his words. We have already seen celestial objects of a large size do strike the Earth with alarming regularity. This coupled with a large, highly-visible comet might lead to the legends of a god-battling sky serpent. Perhaps this is the genesis of the likes of Typhon, Quetzacoatl, Vritra, Jormungandr and their kin.

Where this theory falls down is that it does not explain the everyday encounters with dragons recorded in the past. A comet coiling across the night sky is a fine explanation for a dragon god but not a creature inhabiting a local well and periodically crawling out to suck cow's milk or eat people. Most British dragon legends are not about cosmic events but are about a large and dangerous predator stalking the countryside. In the account from 1274 the writer records a comet *and* a dragon, implying that he knew the difference between the two. Though comets and meteors may have a role to play in dragon lore they cannot explain the whole mystery by a very long way. The roots of the dragon legend may well be set firmly on the Earth.

Earth energies

In China dragons formed part of an ancient geomancy known as *feng shui*. Practitioners of *feng shui* were esoteric surveyors who calculated the best spots to build cities, palaces, tombs and other important buildings. These would be stationed in spots were they would gain the most benefit from the Earth's magnetic currents. These currents could be positive or negative, *yang* and *yin* respectively.

Yang was personified by a male dragon. It followed the routes of high mountains where the dragons lived and flowed along lines where they moved. These were *lung mei* or dragon paths. Keeping the balance between *yin* and *yang* meant that roads, buildings and other manmade contrivances had to be carefully placed.

The success or otherwise of a whole dynasty was believed to rest on the correct burial of the dynasty's founder. Powerful emperors employed geomancers to channel the *lung mei* towards Beijing, the seat of power. No building, except those pertaining to the Emperor himself, were allowed to be built along these paths.

Some Westerners, including author John Michell, think a similar belief used to flourish in ancient Britain. Michell thinks a dragon worship cult flourished here and its members were aware of lines of energy running through the earth. They erected temples accordingly along these lines. When Christianity arrived the clergy attempted to vanquish the old religion by placing their own temples on the sites of the pagan ones. These temples and the lines they follow can be traced by looking for dragon- and serpent-related imagery in the landscape.

Michell identified a number of such 'Michael lines'. The longest line in the British Isles runs 200 miles from St Michael's Mount in Cornwall to Bury St Edmunds in Suffolk. Dragon lore and dragon-related iconography can be found all along it. Starting in the west St Michael's Mount. St Michael was one of the dragon-slaying saints. The area was also a sacred megalithic site. The line then runs through The Hurlers, three prehistoric stone circles on Bodmin

Moor. Legend has it that they were serpents turned to stone by a saint.

Going into neighbouring Devon, we find St Michael's Church on Brent Tor on the edge of Dartmoor. Brent Tor is another huge outcrop of rock believed to have once been the site of pagan worship. Further into Devon we find another St Michael's Church in Cadbury. You will recall that a dragon once made its lair in the ruins of Cadbury Castle that overlooks the church and flew each night to Dolbury hill.

Moving into Somerset some twenty miles away we find the line runs through Trull. A dragon was supposedly slain here and there is another St Michael's Church. A window in the church shows saints George, Michael and Margaret.

Five miles on is Creech St Michael, then Ling where dragons decorate the pews. The ruins of another St Michael's Church sit atop a manmade mound called Burrowbridge Mump. St Michael's at Othery has a porch decorated with a carved dragon.

Still in Somerset Glastonbury Tor is on the line. No prizes for guessing that the ruined chapel at its summit is dedicated to St Michael. Serpentine paths spiral to the summit.

Opposite: *The tower of St Michael's church, Brent Tor.*

Right: *Glastonbury Tor with the tower of St Michael's chapel.*

Photographs by Bob Trubshaw.

The line then passes through Stoke St Michael in the parish of Frome before crossing the border into Dorset. In Dorset it passes through Avebury and its serpent circles of stone.

Ogbourn St George is the next location and has a church dedicated to St George.

According to Paul Newman in his 1979 book *The Hill of the Dragon*, Ogbourn St George is a prehistoric site connected with sun worship. Ogmios is a Gaulish god shown with chains connecting his tongue to a band of happy followers. This may indicate eloquence. He is also associated with the sun and is supposed to look sunburned. Here he is juxtaposed with the Christian St George at Ogbourn.

Finally the line ends at Bury St Edmunds and the prehistoric site of Castle Mound. In the Abbey lie the remains of Edmund the king and martyr.

Oddly Michell's work was largely forgotten until it was revisited in the 1989 book *The Sun and the Serpent* by Paul Broadhurst and Hamish Miller.

At Kilpeck Church in Herefordshire the south doorway is a veritable zoo of dragons and serpents. It drew the following outburst from Bernard of Clairvaux, founder of the Cistercian Order in the twelfth century:

> 'For God's sake, if men are not ashamed of these follies, why at least do they not shrink from the expense?'

What is the nature of these supposed lines of power? The word ley was first used in Alfred Watkins's book *The Old Straight Track* in 1925. Watkins showed that Roman roads usually followed much earlier tracks that criss-cross Britain and were already ancient by the time the Romans arrived. He noted how standing stones, burial mounds, beacons, temples and other ancient sites could be aligned in what he called 'leys' or ancient tracks. Watkins did not think that there was anything esoteric about this. His theory was purely utilitarian. He thought that they were trade routes where flint, salt and metal were transported.

In 1969 Michell, in his book *The View Over Atlantis*, ventured that they were lines of actual energy that the ancients knew how to utilise. Standing stones could be seen as stone pylons for tapping into this energy in some way. The energy was symbolised by a coiling serpent or dragon.

The Greeks believed in a fifth element (after water, air, fire and earth) they called *pneuma*. Medieval alchemists referred to it as the *quintessence*. The Norse called it *ond* and the Celts *nwyvr* or *nwyfre*. In modern Welsh *nwyf* means energy and *nwyfriant* means vigour. *Nwyvr* is quite comparable with both wyvern and gwiber.

Barddas, a collection of ancient Welsh bardic texts collected and published in 1866 describes the elements as follows:

> 'Calas; fluidity; breath; uvel and nwyvre. From calas is every corporeity, namely the earth and every hard thing; from fluidity are moisture and flux; from breath are every wind, breeze, respiration and air; from uvel are all heat; fire and light; and from nwyvre every life and motion, every spirit, every soul of man, and from its union with other elements, other living beings.'

Linguistically *nwyvre* would seem to be related to the Indo-European *wed* meaning water. The Gallic word *vobero* means underground water. This links appropriately with diviners who search for underground water. We could also link this with water being the element that dragons were most associated with. Could these energy lines actually refer to underground watercourses?

It is easy to imagine the geomancer divining for water then thrusting his staff into the earth where he has found it. The staff becomes a spear or sword in legend. Man taming the chaos of nature becomes man fighting the primal serpent in later Christianisation. Another interpretation is that the early Christian hero, transfixing a serpent with his sword, is earthing the energy thus controlling it.

In the 1950s Austrian-born psychiatrist Wilhelm Reich claimed to have discovered a kind of primal energy present in all living things as well as the atmosphere. Reich said that this energy could be accumulated and used for healing purposes. He christened it 'orgone' and claimed it was blue in colour. This is interesting, as the ancient Chinese believed that the azure dragon enshrined the east in geomancy. Blue is also the colour most associated with water.

Appealing as these theories are, they still fall very short of explaining all dragon lore and, in particular, the modern day dragon sightings we shall be looking at later.

Fossil bones

In the 1670s natural historian Robert Plot unearthed a massive bone. He believed it to be the thigh bone of a giant. Ninety years later Richard Brookes – a rural doctor who devoted much of his life to natural history and the rest of it to fishing – examined the knee joint and came to the conclusion that it was the fossilised scrotum of a giant! Accordingly, he named the bone *Scrotum humanum*. It was, in fact, the leg-bone of the flesh-eating dinosaur *Megalosaurus bucklandi* – a nine metre predator that stalked England in the Jurassic and early Cretaceous eras.

There are many cases where the bones of dinosaurs and other prehistoric animals have been mistaken for the remains of legendary creatures. One can readily imagine the impact of finding the massive bones of a dinosaur would have had on early peoples with no knowledge of such creatures. Some believe that this is where we can trace the genesis of the dragon legends.

Beginning in the British Isles, we can find that even the most mundane and common fossil can elicit legends, and they do not have to be of a great size. The common fossilised shells of the extinct cephalopods known as ammonites were often believed to be the remains of serpents. These marine relatives of the modern nautilus lived in spiralled shells. They ranged in size from less than a centimetre to two metres in diameter – females dwarfing males. They became extinct at the end of the Cretaceous epoch some 65 million years ago. It seems that the closely-related nautilus survived because it lived in deep waters less affected by whatever global events destroyed much life at the end of this epoch.

Ammonites take their name from the Latin *cornu Ammonis* – the 'horns' of Zeus Ammon, that is Zeus with a ram's head. Zeus was said to have disguised himself as a ram in Egypt while fleeing the dragon Typhon. (Yet another dragon link!)

In Ireland it was believed that ammonites were the victims of St Patrick in the fifth century, who was said to have driven all snakes out of the 'Emerald Isle'. The fossils confirmed this legend, as those snakes that did not leave Ireland were petrified, beheaded and left in the rocks for all to see as a demonstration of God's power.

These fossils were often called 'snake stones', and legends akin to that of St Patrick are found in other areas rich in ammonite fossils. One such area is Whitby in North Yorkshire. Here the cliffs date from the Jurassic, when ammonites reached their zenith in both species and number. They are preserved in great numbers and are associated with St Hilda. Hilda was a Saxon abbess who founded Whitby Abbey in the fourth century. According to legend, the cliffs were over-run with serpents until St Hilda turned them to stone. Her prayers caused them to fall headless from the cliff tops.

Similar legends are woven around St Kenya at Keynsham in Avon. The same Jurassic rock that composes the cliffs at Whitby is found here.

The craft of carving snakes heads on ammonites and selling them off as relics to religious travellers was popular in Whitby. Michael G. Bassett notes in his book *Formed Stones, Folklore and Fossils* that the type specimen for the ammonite species *Dactylioceras commune* is actually a snake-stone with a carved head. Most of the Whitby ammonites are of this species. Such was the popularity of this kind of fakery that the snake-stone became one of the town's emblems during the sixteenth and seventeenth centuries. They featured on coins, and on the council's coat of arms, where three of them still appear today.

Snake-stones were believed to be potent charms against the bite of venomous creatures. The stones were soaked in water, then the bitten person or animal was given the water to drink. They were also worn like amulets to ward off snakes, and as cures for blindness and impotence. We can see here the link back to the accounts of dragons such as the Greek drackon and the South East Asian naga, being sharp eyed, and also the belief in these dragons as fertility symbols.

Many British dragons – such as the infamous Lambton worm – were known for their love of milk. Lesser serpents were also supposed to be addicted to milk, and there are tales of farmers having to pluck suckling snakes from the udders of sleeping cows. Welsh gwibers were thought to grow from ordinary snakes that suckled a woman's milk. Fossil sea urchins were often thought to be magical 'serpent eggs', and were placed on shelves in dairies to prevent the milk from turning sour.

These magic eggs were known as *ovum anguinum* – stony snake's eggs – and were first recorded in Pliny the Elder's (AD 23–79) *Natural History*. They were supposedly formed by the froth that emanated from a mass of entwined (mating?) snakes at midsummer. The snakes would toss the stone egg into the air. If caught on a cloth before it hit the ground it would have great magical powers.

The village of Kilve in Somerset has a legend about a dragon called 'Blue Ben' who was supposed to be Satan's steed. His skull was discovered and placed in Taunton Museum. The relic was actually the skull of an *Ichthyosaur* – a group of marine reptiles contemporary with the dinosaurs. These fish-eating reptiles superficially resembled dolphins, and ranged in size from 1.5 metres to 12 metres. Doubtless, to those who discovered the skull, with its massive eyes and long tooth studded jaw, it was truly horrific and unlike any animal they knew of – save for a dragon.

Exotic reptiles

In the days before television and general literacy people knew very little about wildlife. All kinds of outlandish beliefs existed about British wildlife let alone creatures from other countries. Bestiaries existed but their illustrations were, in the main, done by people who never seen the exotic animals described within. The drawings were based on second- or third-hand accounts.

Some travellers such as Crusaders or merchants may have encountered exotic reptiles. Some were brought back to Britain and it is known that crocodiles and large snakes were exhibited at the menagerie in the Tower of London. Could some of these have started legends after breaking free?

People have a habit of exaggeration, which is how many 'monsters' are created. We have always wanted the animals who share our planet to be larger, and fiercer and smarter than they actually are. The more dangerous we perceive the animal to be, then the greater the tales that we weave around it. Few carnivores are as dangerous to man as many people would like to think. It is, however, fitting that reptiles are one of the few groups of animals with a real tendency towards gigantism, and that the crocodile is one of the few genuine man-eaters.

To be fair, only two of the twenty-three extant species of crocodilian regularly attack humans. These are the Nile crocodile (*Crocodylus niloticus*) and the Indopacific crocodile (*C. porosus*). But these account for five thousand human deaths a year – far more than all attacks by shark, big cat or bear combined. Of vertebrates, only humans themselves kill more.

These are truly spectacular predators and have been recorded to have killed prey as formidable as lions, tigers, hippo, rhino, water buffalo and even sharks. A really big crocodile can reach nine metres or more and weigh in at three tons. No other animal inspires such a primal dread in humanity as the crocodile. The armour plated hide, the massive jaws furnished with dagger-like teeth coupled with their huge size (up to nine metres) make crocodiles excellent prototypes for dragons.

The monster exhibited in Durham in 1568 was almost certainly a crocodile. The event is recorded in the St Nicholas Register:

> 'A certain Italian brought into the city of Durham, on
> the 11th day of the above said, a very great, strange
> and monstrous serpent, in length sixteen feet, in
> quantity and dimensions greater than a horse; which
> was taken by special police in Aethiopia, within The
> Turk's dominions. But before it was killed it hade
> devoured (as credibly thought) more than 1,000
> persons and destroyed a whole country.'

One of the most celebrated English dragon legends seems to have its beginnings with an escaped crocodile. A translation of a document dating to 1402 runs:

> 'Close to the town of Bures, near Sudbury, there has lately appeared, to the great hurt of the countryside, a dragon, vast in body, with a crested head, teeth like a saw, and a tail extending to an enormous length. Having slaughtered the shepherd of a flock it devoured many sheep. There came forth in order to shoot at him with arrows the work men of the lord on whose estate he had concealed himself, being Sir Richard Waldergrave, Knight: but the dragon's body, though struck by the archers, remained unhurt, for the arrows bounced off his back as if it were iron or hard rock. Those arrows that fell upon the spine of his back gave out a sound, as they struck it a ringing or tinkling sound, just as if they had hit a brazen plate, then flew away off by reason of the hide of this great beast being impenetrable. Thereupon, in order to destroy him, all the country people around were summoned. But when the dragon saw that he was again about to be assailed with arrows, he fled into a marsh or mere and there hid himself among the long reeds, and was no more seen.'

The neighbouring town of Wormingford claim that this story happened there and not in Bures. In the Wormingford version the dragon was in fact a 'crockadrill' brought back by Richard I (1157–99; reigned from 1183), from the Third Crusade for his menagerie in the Tower of London. The reptile escaped and made its way through Essex to the River Stour. Its reign of terror was final curbed by Sir George de la Haye, when he slew it after a fearful battle in a field called 'Bloody Meadows'. In the Wormingford story the monster is described as having short limbs with great nails or talons and a long curved tail.

The descriptions from both legends do indeed sound remarkably like a crocodile. These creatures were brought back to England and displayed. If one did escape into rural areas it would have caused panic. To folk who were used only to wolves and bears at the worst a six to nine metre reptile would have surely seemed like a nightmare from hell!

Snakes hold a special fascination for man, perhaps because of their 'alienness'. Their vermiform-bodies have no limbs, and their eyes no lids. They have no ears and 'hear' by picking-up vibrations – via their bodies – through the ground. Many types are venomous and the idea of such small (in the main) animals being so formidably armed is disturbing. Humanity fears that which is different, and this fear has manifest in many different ways from the snake-veneration of the Aztecs, to the disgusting rattlesnake round-ups of the southern United States, where thousands of snakes are captured and cruelly slaughtered in the name of 'fun' by worthless red necked scum. It is unsurprising then, that snakes have their part to play in the rich tapestry of dragon lore.

One of the most formidable of dragon kin – the basilisk – may have had its genesis in a very real group of snakes – the cobras. As you may recall from Chapter One, the basilisk was vulnerable to only two creatures, the rooster and the weasel. Weasels belong to a group of mammals called *Mustelids*. These include stoats, otters, badgers, wolverines and martens. The group bears a striking similarity to the *Viverrids* or mongooses. This is a case of convergent or parallel evolution, where two distinct groups of animals develop to resemble each other as a consequence of fulfilling similar ecological niches. There are differences. *Mustelids* have greater variation in form, and grow larger than *Viverrids*, but the weasel and the common mongoose are sufficiently alike for confusion to arise between the two. The cobra's hood could also add to the legend by being distorted into the basilisk's crown.

Another factor in the legend of the basilisk seems to lie with the black mamba (*Dendroaspis polyepis*) – a large and highly venomous snake of sub-Saharan Africa. This snake can reach four metres in length, and is renowned for its aggressiveness. When in a warning display it can rear up to the height of a man and, unlike most other snakes, it will actively pursue and attack anything that it perceives as a threat. Most snakes strike only once. The black mamba strikes repeatedly, and has a potent neurotoxin (nerve paralysing) venom. It has been recorded on many occasions that black mambas shedding their skin sometimes retain a flap of old dead skin upon their head. This strongly resembles the crest of a cockerel, and may well have led to legends of crested-serpents – both in Africa and elsewhere – via visiting foreigners.

But what of the other factors in the basilisk legend? It seems that these also have explanations within the realm of the natural rather than the supernatural. The miraculous egg-laying cockerel is not so fantastic as it at first sounds. There is a disease in fowl that causes a hen's ovaries to become infected. This prevents the production of the female hormone oestrogen. Oestrogen controls feminine characteristics, and when these are prevented from developing, masculine traits appear. These include developing a comb and wattle, crowing and attempting to mount hens. If the victim recovers, it returns to its former feminine self and may lay once more; *ergo* a cock that lays eggs.

How about the snakes that sometimes slithered out of hens eggs, to the mortification and horror of medieval cooks? Snake eggs are leathery-shelled and not at all like birds eggs, so confusion between the two – or deliberate mischief (a jester switching hen eggs for snake eggs for example) – is unlikely. The explanation is almost as grim as the original legend! Chickens often suffer from round-worms (*Ascaris*). These endoparasitic, internal creatures are mainly passed out in the bird's droppings but they can on occasion enter the reproductive-tract and be incorporated into an egg. In times past – when there were no stringent hygiene laws – this would have occurred far more often than today. Round worms can measure up to forty centimetres and one could readily imagine the terror evoked by cracking open an egg to find a writhing 'basilisk' within!

An exotic snake may explain the legend of the dragon of St Leonard's Forest in Sussex. In 1614 a bizarre creature appeared in the forest, much to the alarm of the locals. John Trundle published a broadsheet describing the phenomenon in full:

> In Sussex there is a pretty market towne called
> Horsham, near which is a forest called St. Leonards
> Forrest, and there is a vast and unfrequented place,
> heahie, vaultie, full of unwholsome shades and
> overgrown hollows where this serpent is thought to be
> bred, certain and too true, that there it yet lives,
> within 3 or 4 miles compass are its usual haunts,
> oftentimes at a place called Fay-Gate, and it hath
> been seene within half a mile of Horsham, a wonder
> no doubt, most, terrible and noisome to the
> inhabitants thereabouts.
>
> There is always in his track or path left a glutinous
> and slimie matter (as by a small simailitude we may
> percive in a snail) which is very courpt and offensive
> to the scent, insomuch they percive the air to be

putrified withal which must needs be very dangerous; for though the corruption of it cannot strike the outward parts of a man, unless heated into the blood, yet by receving it into any part of our breathing organs (the nose or mouth) it is by authoritie of all authors, writing in that kinde, mortall and deadlie; as one thus saith: 'Nosia Serpentane est admits sangine Pestis (Lucan).

The Serpent or Dragon as some call it, is reputed to be nine feete or rather more in length, and shaped almost in the form of the axle-tree of a cart, a quantitie of thickness in the middest, and somewhat smaller at both ends. The former part which he shoots forth as a necke is supposed to be an ell long, with a white ring as it were of scales about it. The scales along his back seem to be blackish and so much as is descovered under his bellie apereth to be red; for I speak of no nearer a description than a reasonable ocular distance; for coming too neare it hath already been too dearlie pay'd for as you shall hear herafter.

It is likewise descovered to have large feete, but the eye may be there deceived, for some suppose that serpents have no feet but glide along upon certain ribbes and scales, which both defend them, from the upper part of the throat, unto the lower part of their bellie, and also cause them to move much faster, for so this doth and rids away, as we call it, as fast as a man can run. He is of counternence very proud, at the sight or hearing of man or cattle, he will raise his neck upright, and seem to listen and looke about him with great arrogance. There are likewise on either side of him discovered two great bunches, so big as a large foote ball, and as some think will grow into wings, but God I hope will so defend the poor people of the neighbourhood, that he shall be destroyed before he grow so fledge. He will cast venom about 4 roddes from him, so by woefull experience, it was proved on the bodies of a man and a woman coming that way, who aferwards were found dead, being poysoned and very much swelled, but not preyed upon; likewise a man going to chase it and as he imagined to destroy it with great mastiff dogs were both killed and he himself had to return with haste to preserve his own life. Yet this is to be noted that the dogs were not preyed upon, but slaine and left whole- for his food is thought to be for the most part in a conie warren which he most frequents, and it is found to be much scanted and impaired in the increase it had wont to afford. These persons whose names are hear under-printed have seen this serpent, besides divers others, as the carrier at Horsham, who lieth at the White Horse in Southwark, and who can certifie the truth of all that hath herein been related.

John Steele,
Christopher Holder,
And a widow woman dwelling at Fay-Gate.

The description of the serpent 'raising up his head' sounds very like a cobra rearing up in a threat posture. The fact that its victims remained uneaten, while the serpent fed on smaller animals such as rabbits (conies) also points to a venomous snake. The 'bunches' in the creature's middle may have been reference to a sighting just after the snake had fed, lending it a fatter appearance about the middle. As for the slime and fouled-air, some snakes will spout foul-smelling excreta from their cloaca if alarmed. The snake was indeed probably a cobra that had its genesis in one of the animal collections at the time and escaped into the area. The reports began in August and only lasted a few months before the cold winter would have killed any tropical reptile at large.

It is not the venomous snakes that cause the most awe in us however, but the giant constrictors. Constricting snakes – the boas and pythons – are the largest snakes alive, although not all reach excessive lengths (some are little over half a metre long). Five species are known to exceed six metres in length. These are:

Python reticulatus, the reticulated python at 33 feet (10.65 metres)

Eunectes murinus, the anaconda at 29 feet (9.35 metres)

Moreli amethistina, the amethystine python at 28 feet (9.03 metres)

Python sabae, the African rock python at 25 feet (8.06 metres)

Python molurus, the Indian python at 25 feet (8.06 metres)

Python molurus bivittatus, the Burmese python at 26.5 feet (8.55 metres).

If such a creature got loose in the British countryside in bygone days one could well imagine the terror they would inspire. Constricting snakes would make a good analogue for the worm type of dragon. One could survive for several months during summer – enough time to enter into legend. I fancy several stories such as the one at Fittleworth have their genesis in this way.

An unknown species

In his 1979 book *The Flight of Dragons,* Peter Dickinson attempts something not done since Charles Gould's 1886 book *Mythical Monsters* – that is, to explain fire-breathing, winged dragons as real animals within the known zoological framework.

Impressed by the universality of dragon-legends, Dickinson believed that they had a basis in fact. The main stumbling block was the sheer size of dragons – animals that after all were supposed to have flown. Looking at mediaeval reconstructions of dragons, he reckoned their weight to be around nine tonnes (20,000 pounds). In order to be able to fly by the muscular power of its wings, a dragon of this weight would need a wingspan of over 180 metres – far too massive to be real. And how could an animal possibly breathe out fire? These problems seemed insurmountable, until a chance viewing of the crash of the *Hindenburg.*

> '... one day I happened to see on television an old newsreel film of the wreck of the airship Hindenburg, an almost in a flash all my ideas changed. As I watched the monstrous shape crumpling and tumbling in fiery fragments, with the smoke clouds swirling above, I said to myself, it flamed and it fell, and my mind made the leap to Jordanus. All the pieces I had been considering shook themselves into a different shape. I saw that the Hindenburg was not just a very big machine which flew it was a machine which could fly only because it was very big. Other answers slotted into place.

Dragons could fly because most of their bodies were hollow, and filled with a lighter-than-air gas.

Dragons needed an enormous body to hold enough gas to provide lift for the total weight of the beast.

Dragons did not need enormous wings, because they used them only for propulsion and manoeuvring.

Dragons breathed fire because they had to. It was a necessary part of their specialised mode of flight.'

Dickinson's theory held that dragons evolved from large fast moving carnivorous dinosaurs like *Tyrannosaurus rex*. They developed huge, chambered stomachs that they filled with hydrogen gas, thus achieving flight. The hydrogen was formed from a mixture of hydrochloric acid in the gut and calcium from the bones of their victims, and controlled partial-digestion of their own bone structure. The calcium taken from their own bones was being constantly replaced with a regular intake of limestone. This may explain the dragon's legendary love of lairing in caves.

The vast-body was filled with this gas, and the animal acted – in essence – as a living dirigible. As any chemist will know, hydrogen mixed with oxygen is highly flammable. This is where the dragon's most famous attribute – its fiery breath – came into play. Dragons needed to breathe fire in order to control their flight. To rise, they filled their gas-bag stomachs, and to descend they burned-off gas by breathing it out – possibly with a chemical catalyst, as fire.

The fiery-breath doubtless doubled up as a formidable weapon – a punishing jet of flame with which to destroy prey and as a display to other members of its species. A similar weapon is employed by the bombardier beetle (*Brachinus*) that spews a jet of boiling chemicals at its enemies. The two chemical components are produced from different glands, and do not reach high temperatures until outside of the beetle's body.

The wings were formed from the extended ribcage – much like that of the modern lizard *Draco volans*, a small gliding species often called the 'flying dragon'. These were covered with a bat-like membrane and were used in navigating the animal in flight.

Dickinson also believes that he can explain some of the more esoteric aspects of dragon legends. The cult of dragon-worship would have sprung up from primitive people's fear of such a

*Lighter than air b
Ian Brown*

terrifying creature. The famous 'dragon hoards' would have been built from offerings made to appease the monsters. Dickinson says that dragons would have used gold as a nesting material as it is non-combustible and fairly soft. Their fondness of virgins may have its genesis in human worship and sacrifice of highborn victims, perhaps born and raised specifically as sacrifices to dragons.

The theory also provides a good reason why there are no known dragon fossils. In life, a thick mucous-lining in the stomach-walls kept the powerful hydrochloric acid needed to produce hydrogen in check. After death, the mucous-lining was no longer generated, and the acid destroyed the animal's body. The creature literally digested itself. Hence no dragon bones and no dragon fossils. It is for this very reason that Dickinson's theory is impossible to prove. In effect he is foisted by his own petard, and his wonderful theory must – for the time being – remain just a tantalising possibility.

No one theory is likely to explain all dragon legends. Dragon lore is a very old and complex tapestry involving many strands. The word 'dragon' has meant a lot of different things to many people through the centuries. When all these meanings are pulled together into one the dragon becomes all the more awe inspiring.

Paranormal phenomena

So far we have considered the possibility that dragons were some kind of physical creature. Perhaps we are barking up the wrong tree. Can such a magical, powerful beast be confined to mere flesh and bone? Could the origins of dragons lie outside the boundaries of standard zoology or even cryptozoology?

There are a legion of cryptozoological cases that cannot be seen within a purely zoological framework. Pure cryptozoology is the study of mystery animals, those erroneously believed to be extinct, and those unknown to modern science. But reports of unknown animals rub shoulders with cases and creatures that are so bizarre that they refuse to be slotted into a 'natural' order. These include monsters that appear and disappear in front of witnesses, creatures that seem immune to any weapons, beasts that rear their heads amidst other unexplained phenomena, and things that seem to generate fear at truly incredible levels.

This latter power is possessed by perhaps the most famous of living worms, the Loch Ness Monster. In the final chapter we will examine the monster and its kin throughout the world in detail, but for now we will confine ourselves to the stranger aspects of Scotland's most celebrated denizen.

One of the earliest and most famous of twentieth century sightings occurred on 22nd July 1933. Mr George Spicer – proprietor of a firm of London tailors – and his wife were enjoying a motoring holiday in the Highlands. There enjoyment was rudely interrupted at 4 o'clock in the afternoon as they drove from Dores to Foyers via the winding loch-side road.

> 'We were midway between Dores and Foyers on the
> south bank of the loch when my wife exclaimed,
> 'What on earth is that?' I was looking ahead as my
> wife spoke; I observed the most extraordinary form of
> an animal crossing the road. It was horrible – an
> abomination.
>
> First we saw an undulating sort of neck, a little thicker
> than an elephant's trunk. It did not move in the usual
> reptilian fashion but, with three arches in its neck, it
> shot across the road until a ponderous body about
> four feet high came into view.

When we reached the part of the road it had crossed, we stopped, but there was no sign of it. It had been a loathsome sight. It seems futile to describe it because it was like nothing I have read about or seen. It was terrible. Its colour, so far as the body was concerned, could be called a dark elephant grey. It looked like a huge snail with a long neck. I reported the affair to various scientific bodies all of who seemed incredulous. I am willing to take an oath, and so is my wife, that we saw this Loch Ness beast.'

Spicer estimated the monster to have been twenty-five to thirty feet (7.5 to 9 metres) long. From his description it is obvious that the creature badly frightened him. He later called for the loch to be dynamited.

This recoiling of the mind has been shared by many other witnesses. Mr Richard Jenkyns and his wife saw the horror from their loch-side house on the 30th September 1974. The couple watched the monster through binoculars for half an hour. It seemed to be around eighteen metres in length. The monster had a lasting effect on them. Later Richard commented:

'I felt the beast was obscene. This feeling of obscenity still persists and the whole thing put me in mind of a gigantic stomach with a long writhing gut attached.'

Mrs Greta Finlay – an Inverness housewife – had similar feelings toward the thing she encountered at close range on 20th August 1952. She had gone fishing with her young son, and was on the north-east shore of the loch near Aldourie pier, off Tor Point.

'I was sitting outside the caravan when I heard a continual splashing in the water. After several moments passed and realising this was not the usual wash from a boat I walked round. To my surprise I saw what I believe to be the Loch Ness Monster. My son and I stood looking at this creature in amazement. Although I was terrified, we stood and watched it until it submerged, which it did very quickly causing waves to break on the shore. We had an excellent view, as it was so close to the shore. Its skin was dark in colour and looked very tough. The neck was long and held erect. The head was about the same width as the neck. There were two projections from it, each with a blob at the end. This was not a pleasant experience. I certainly never want to see the monster again.'

Mrs Finlay was interviewed by the late Tim Dinsdale – perhaps the greatest 'Nessie'-hunter of them all. She confessed to him that she had been paralysed with fear, and that her son had been so utterly horrified, that he had given up fishing all together.

In 1899 a flamboyant character arrived in Inverness. He purchased the brooding Boleskine House on the shores of Loch Ness for twice the amount the building was worth, becoming the self-styled 'Laird of Boleskine'. The man was Aleister Crowley, and he had good reasons for paying over the odds for the remote forbidding house.

Crowley was born in Leamington, Warwickshire, in 1875. Rebelling against his ultra-strict Christian upbringing, he became the most flamboyant and colourful character in British occultism. His magical and sexual experimentation shocked the prudish Victorian society. Crowley revelled in this and wove an intricate web of myths about himself.

He chose Boleskine on account of its occult architecture. Previously he had scoured Britain for an abode to suit his needs and found none. Once in Boleskine he intended to carry out the ritual of Abra-Melin – an ancient rite that took eighteen months to perform.

The ritual harkened back to the 1400s and had been translated by a Jewish scholar called Abriham the Jew, from a North African manuscript. Abriham was wandering the Middle-East looking for true magicians from whom to learn. He finally came upon a wizened mage called Abra-Melin who passed the rite onto him. It dealt with the summoning of demonic forces. The ritual demanded idiosyncratic architecture, which Crowley had previously tried to replicate in his London flat. Though not having the desired effect strange things happened there. In the 'Great Beast's' own words:

> 'During this time magical phenomena were of
> constant occurrence. I had two temples in my flat;
> one white, the walls being lined with six huge
> mirrors, each six feet by eight; the other black a mere
> cupboard in which stood an altar supported by the
> figure of a Negro standing on his hands. The presiding
> genius of this place was a human skeleton, which I
> fed from time to time with blood, small birds and the

like. The idea was to give it life, but I never got
further than causing the bones to become covered in
a viscous slime.'

Yet more happened at Crowley's flat, apparently on account of the
occult décor:

'The demons connected with Abra-Melin do not wait
to be evoked; they come unsought. One night Jones
and I were out to dinner. I noticed while leaving the
white temple that the latch of the Yale lock had not
caught. Accordingly, I pulled the door to and tested it.
As we went out, we noticed semi-solid shadows on
the stairs; the whole atmosphere was vibrating with
the forces we had been using. (We were trying to
condense them into sensible images.) When we came
back nothing had been disturbed in the flat; but the
temple door was wide open, the furniture disarranged
and some of the symbols flung about the room. We
restored order and then observed that the semi-
materialised beings were marching around the room
in almost unending procession.

When I finally left the flat for Scotland, it was found
that there was no way to take the mirrors out except
by way of the black temple. This had, of course been
completely dismantled before the workmen arrived.
But the atmosphere remained and two of them were
put out of action for several hours. It was almost a
weekly experience, by the way, to hear of the casual
callers fainting or being seized with dizziness, cramp
or apoplexy on the staircase. It was a long time before
those rooms were re-let. People fled instinctively at
the presence of something uncanny. Similarly, later
on, when I gave up my rooms on Victoria Street, a
pushing charlatan thought to better himself by taking
them. With this object he went to see them. A few
seconds later he was leaping headlong down the five
flights of stairs, screaming in terror. He had sufficient
genuine sensitiveness to feel the forces, without
possessing the knowledge, courage and will required
to turn them to account, or even endure their impact.'

Crowley's attempts to perform the ritual at Boleskine failed. No one knows quite why, but the rite was never completed. The semi-formed shadows that he evoked in London seemed to have been called again, however. John Symonds – his biographer – recounts that the house's lodge and terrace became peopled by shadowy shapes. The place seemed to have a strange and violent effect on people. A workman employed to renovate the villa went berserk and attacked Crowley, who had to knock the man out and lock him in a coal-shed. His lodge-keeper – who had been a teetotaller – went on a three-day drinking-binge and tried to murder his own wife and children. Crowley finally left in 1918 but some believe he left something behind.

Subsequent owners of Boleskine have also reported disturbances. Musician and former member of the supergroup Led Zeppelin, Jimmy Page brought the house in the 1970s. His friend and custodian of Boleskine, Malcolm Dent, has experienced the house's dark side on several occasions:

> 'Most of the oddities occurred during upheavals in the
> house. I am not talking about wallpapering, but
> structural alterations. Any time there was any thing
> major, it was almost as though the house didn't like
> it. If we didn't get on with the job and get it finished,
> something would let us know about it. We would be
> wakened up during the night with heavy doors
> banging all over the place and carpets and rugs being
> rolled up. It was though it was a reminder to get on
> quickly and get the job over.'

Another time, Malcolm and some friends, saw a statue of the Devil rise up from a mantelpiece, float to the ceiling then smash to the floor. The most horrifying event happened early one morning when the disturbances reached a crescendo. Malcolm spent a night huddled in fear as what sounded like some huge beast hammered at in door making an awful sound. It did not retreat until daybreak.

Modern day wizard and Fortean investigator Tony 'Doc' Sheils was at Loch Ness when he made the acquaintance of a man named Patrick Kelly. Kelly claimed to have photographed a lake monster in Lough Leane, in 1981. This however was not the most fantastic of his claims.

He said that he was a direct descendent of Edward Kelly, the notorious scryer of Dr John Dee. Dee was the court magician to

137

Queen Elizabeth I, and claimed to 'speak with the dead' via a young medium whom he had trained.

The modern day Kelly also claimed his father, Laurence, had met Aleister Crowley in Paris in 1933 shortly after he had left the Abbey of Thelema. Crowley told Laurence that he was very interested in the Loch Ness Monster – whose first major flap of the twentieth century had just started.

Finally Patrick Kelly and his father both claim to have seen the Loch Ness Monster on 1st May 1969 close to Boleskine. Fantastic assertions indeed – but at least for this last one there may be some evidence. In June of the same year, three American students were exploring the seventeenth century cemetery below Boleskine House. They came upon a curious object. It was an old tapestry wrapped around a conch-shell. The tapestry was decorated with serpent-like symbols embroidered in gold thread. It measured four feet by five feet (1.3 by 1.6 metres), and seemed to be old and threadbare. There were reddish-stains at each corner, as if objects had been placed there.

All in all it looked like an altar-cloth. The shell was about five inches (12 cm) long, white and inscribed with two parallel grooves and a lotus blossom. When blew it produced a harsh braying sound. The objects were taken to the Victoria and Albert Museum to be studied by experts. The tapestry was latter identified as being Turkish in origin. The snake-like symbols were Turkish script for 'serpent'. We should also note that today Lake Van in the east of Turkey, is said to be inhabited by a dragon.

The idea that the Loch Ness Monster was a malevolent supernatural entity reached its peak some years before in the early 1970s. In 1973 one man believed things had gone on too long, and decided to exorcise Loch Ness. He was the Reverend Dr Donald Ormand. Dr Ormand was perhaps the twentieth century's most renowned exorcist. During his long career he had dealt not just with ghosts and demonic possession, but with latter-day vampires, phantom black dogs and areas of the sea where people were drawn by a strange siren-like urge to drown themselves. These cases, fantastic as they are, pale into children's games, when compared to the doctor's strangest case.

Dr Ormand's first encounter with a lake monster happened in 1967 while on a caravanning holiday on the shores of Long Loch in Ross-shire. He saw a huge aquatic animal with two humps. Not until the following year did Dr Ormand begin to suspect that these monsters were not conventional flesh and blood creatures. In June 1968 he had a far more alarming encounter with a sea-serpent. The reverend was holidaying with his friend Captain Jan Andersen in Norway. While sailing the boat was approached by a huge animal showing two humps. Anderson connected it with the serpent in the Garden of Eden. He told Ormand that these were supernatural beasts that could damage men souls.

He had his ideas backed up in 1972 while attending a meeting of the Organisation of Enquiry into Psychical Disorder in Sweden. An eminent Scandinavian neurologist delivered a report concerning the monster of Lake Storjsson. The report was about the malevolent effect that the monster seemed to have on those who hunted for it, or who had seen it regularly. It resulted in shocking moral degeneration. Similar patterns were found, or so the neurologist claimed, in Irish and Scottish cases.

Ormand drew up a rite from German, Spanish, Roman, Greek, and English sources. On 2nd June 1973 the ritual took place.

> 'I adjure thee, thou ancient serpent, by the judge of
> the quick and the dead, by Him who made thee and
> the world, that thou cloak thyself no more in
> manifestation of prehistoric demons, which henceforth
> shall bring no sorrow to the children of men.'

After the ceremony, Dr Ormand felt drained and fell into a deep sleep. He believed his exorcism to have been a success and subsequently went on to exorcise Lake Storjsson in Sweden. However monsters are still reported in both of these lakes today.

Quite a story, all in all. What are we to make of it? Are these the ramblings of a fundamentalist Christian madman with his worldview set in the Dark Ages, or was the doctor really grappling with some supernatural force in the form of a monster? Exorcism is not confined to Christianity – many other faiths have practising exorcists: Muslim priests cast out *djinn* and pagan wizards and witches drive out malignant spirits with spells. But if these creatures are of paranormal origin just what are they?

There are two schools of thought on this, each with some merit. The first is that they are somehow created by ourselves, unwittingly, through the power of our minds. The second is that they exist independently of us, either unseen on this world, or in some other dimension or reality from whence they occasionally stray.

Let us examine the former theory first. The Buddhist monks of Tibet, Nepal and other parts of the Orient have long claimed to be able to create tangible objects with the power of their minds alone. Through deep concentration, and extreme mental discipline it is said they can create a kind of spirit being – an artificial ghost if you will – that is so convincing that it is often mistaken for a real person or animal. These mind beings are called 'tulpas'. Westerners have experimented with them to varying degrees of success.

Perhaps the most renowned of these was a remarkable Frenchwoman called Dame Alexandra David-Neel. Born in 1868, she lived during a period where women were considered very much as second class citizens and were expected to live their lives as dutiful obedient wives. This makes her 100-year life as an explorer and mystic even more incredible. She travelled extensively in the Himalayas and eventually became a Lama, (the highest ranking Tibetan Buddhist – or Lamaist – priest) in Tibet.

She created a thought form or tulpa herself, with remarkable consequences. She relates the happenings in her book *Magic and Mystery in Tibet*:

> 'I could hardly deny the possibility of visualising and animating a tulpa. Besides having had a few opportunities of seeing thought forms, my habitual incredulity led me to make experiments for myself, and my efforts were attended by some success. In order to avoid being influenced by the forms of the lamaist deities, which I saw daily around me in paintings and images, I chose for my experiment a most insignificant character: a monk, short and fat, of an innocent and jolly type.
>
> I shut myself in doors and proceeded to perform the prescribed concentration of thought and other rites. After a few months the phantom monk was formed. His form grew gradually fixed and lifelike looking. He became a kind of guest, living in my apartment. I then broke my seclusion and started for a tour, with servants and tents.
>
> The monk included himself in the party. Though I lived in the open, riding on horseback for miles each day, the illusion persisted. I saw the far tulpa, now

and then. It was not necessary for me to think of him to make him appear. The phantom preformed various actions of the kind that are natural to travellers and that I had not commanded. For instance, he walked, stopped, looked round him. The illusion was mostly visual, but sometimes I felt as if a robe was lightly rubbing against me, and once a hand seemed to touch my shoulder.

The features which I had imagined, when building my phantom, gradually underwent a change. The fat, chubby-cheeked fellow grew leaner, his face assumed a vaguely mocking, sly, malignant look. He became more troublesome and bold. In brief, he escaped my control.

Once, a herdsman who brought me a present of butter saw the tulpa in my tent and took it for a live lama.

I ought to have let the phenomenon follow its course, but the presence of that unwanted companion began to prove trying on my nerves; it turned into a 'daymare'. Moreover I was beginning to plan my journey to Lhasa, and needed a quiet brain devoid of any other preoccupations, so I decided to dissolve the phantom. I succeeded, but only after six months of hard struggle. My mind creature was tenacious of life.

There are those who think that Alexandra David-Neel's accounts are highly fictionalised and inspired by the works of nineteenth century mystic Madame Blavatsky. Tulpas themselves are not part of Buddhist doctrine. As explained to me by my Buddhist friend Bob Mann, the tulpa is a facet of Himalayan folklore co-opted into the religion locally, in the way religions often tend to absorb local beliefs.

Another remarkable woman who had experience with tulpas was Violet Mary Firth – better known by her pen name of Dion Fortune. In perhaps her best-known work, *Psychic Self-Defence*, she describes how such creatures can be created inadvertently. After being severely wronged, she lay brooding on her bed one night. In a state between sleep and wakefulness, she began to think of Fenris – the demonic wolf who devours Odin in Ragnarok, the death of the gods in Norse myth. After a strange drawing-out feeling from her solar-plexus, she was horrified to see a huge, snarling wolf materialize on the bed next to her.

> 'I knew nothing about the art of making elementals at
> that time, but had accidentally stumbled upon the
> right method – the brooding highly charged with
> emotion, the invocation of the appropriate natural
> force, the condition between sleeping and waking in
> which the etheric double readily extrudes.

> 'I was horrified at what I had done, and knew I was
> in a tight corner and that everything depended on me
> keeping my head. I had enough experience of
> practical occultism to know the thing I had called into
> visible manifestation could be controlled by my will
> provided I did not panic; but if I lost my nerve and it
> got the upper hand, I had a Frankenstein monster to
> cope with.'

She got an idea of the phantom's power the next day, when several of her housemates complained of nightmares about wolves. She came to the conclusion that the wolf was really part of herself, extruded and after revenge. She made the decision to forgo her revenge, and attempt to reabsorb the beast. She called it forth into her room once more.

> 'I obtained an excellent materialization in the half-
> light, and could have sworn a big Alsatian was
> standing there looking at me. It was tangible, even to
> the dog like odour.

'From it to me stretched a shadowy line of ectoplasm, one end was attached to my solar plexus, and the other disappeared in the shaggy fur of its belly, but I could not see the actual point of attachment. I began by an effort of the will and imagination to draw the life out of it along this silver cord, as if sucking lemonade up a straw. The wolf form began to fade, the cord thickened and grew more substantial. A violent emotional upheaval started in myself; I felt the most furious impulses to go berserk and rend and tear anything and anybody that came to hand, like the Malay running amok. I conquered this impulse with an effort, and the upheaval subsided. The wolf form had now faded into a shapeless grey mist. This too was absorbed along the silver cord. The tension relaxed and I found myself bathed in perspiration. That, as far as I know, was the end of the incident.'

Fate magazine ran a story in 1960 written by Nicholas Mamontoff, the son of one of a group of Russian occultists who studied under a Tibetan guru. The mystic had told the 'Brotherhood of the Rising Sun' that Western scientists had never known how powerful the human mind is or what miracles it could work. In 1912 he led the group in an experiment to create an egrigor – another term for a tulpa. One of the Brotherhood had suggested they create a dragon, but the guru suggested that they create something harmless. They decided on a 'Puss in Boots' character, and concentrated on the image for about half an hour. Gradually, a cloud began to form, that condensed into a red-haired cat. Its clothes, however, were ill-formed. The guru suggested that they gave it only boots, eschewing the hat, coat and other items. This improved the creature's clarity:

Within a few moments the features of the cat stabilised and on its hind feet were a pair of Russian boots. The egrigor was motionless and looked like a poorly-developed photograph.

There is evidence that these phantoms of the mind can be created subconsciously. Robin Furman is one of Britain's best known parapsychologists. He runs 'Ghostbusters U.K' – a company that investigates paranormal occurrences such as hauntings, poltergeist outbreaks, possessions and other manifestations. I have met Robin on several occasions and always found him to be honest, likable, wise and deeply-fascinating. Well-respected in his field, Robin has witnessed many strange beings for himself. Robin told me of his own dragon encounter he had as a boy. He suffered an unpleasant childhood at the hands of his violent father. Once – after being sent to bed with a thrashing – he had a very strange visitor.

I looked up to see an enormous dragon walking straight through my bedroom wall. It was green with huge wings. The thing I remember most about it was its tail that it held up in the air in long coils. I wasn't afraid of it. It just walked through my room and out down the corridor. I ran down stairs shouting for my parents to come and look at the dragon but they could not see it.

Perhaps Robin's dragon was an 'unconscious tulpa'. Maybe his subconscious had created a 'guardian' for him in the shape of the biggest, fiercest creature it knew – a dragon.

Another example of involuntary thought-form creation is mentioned in W.Y. Evans-Wentz in the book *The Tibetan Book of the Great Liberation*:

> 'Mediums in the Occident can, while entranced,
> automatically and unconsciously create
> materialisations which are much less palpable than
> the consciously produced tulpas by exuding
> 'ectoplasm' from their own bodies. Similarly, as is
> suggested by instances of phantasms of the living
> reported by psychic research, a thought form may be
> made to emanate from one human mind and by
> hallucinatory perceived by another, although
> possessed of little or no palpableness'.

Further clues to the *gestalt* thought-form can be gleaned from the case of one Franek Kluski. His real name was Teofil Modrzejewski, and from an early age he knew that he was 'different'. As a boy, he claimed to be able to see dead relatives and animals. He also had out-of-body experiences. Importantly, other children with him at the time, claimed to also be able to see 'the dead', as if he were passing on his power to those around him.

When Kluski grew up, he worked partly as an engineer and partly as a professional medium. His speciality was the 'materialization' of spirit-animals, and he seemed to have a whole phantom menagerie at his beck and call. Sitters at his séances saw a big cat like a lioness that would stalk around them, lashing its tail, and leaving behind a strong, acrid smell that lingered for some time. Another beast was christened 'Pithecanthropus' by witnesses after the now-defunct name for the primitive human *Homo erectus*. The creature seemed part-ape and part-man. The brute seemed benevolent in nature but possessed vast strength. One witness, Colonel Norbert Ocholowicz noted:

> 'It could easily move a heavy bookcase filled with
> books through the room, carry a sofa over the heads
> of the sitters, or lift the heaviest persons, in their
> chairs, to the height of a tall person.'

Other sitters felt the 'ape-man' rub its furry hide against their cheeks, and lick their hands, revealing that the creature could be felt as well as seen. It too left behind a foul odour.

Another member of Kluski's 'Zoo' was an owl-like bird that would apparently materialise in mid-air and fly noisily around the room.

On 30th August 1919, at a séance in Warsaw, the bird was photographed perching on Kluski's head. The shot revealed the bird to be remarkably similar to *Caprimulgus europaeus*, the European nightjar.

It seemed as if Kluski was tapping into what I have called the International Monster Template or IMT. Certain monster archetypes seem to turn up again and again in every culture – such as dragons, lake and sea monsters, yeti and sasquatch, the thunderbird and the roc, fairy and goblin lore (including its modern manifestation of 'alien' abduction), the alien big cats that stalk the UK, and the phantom black dogs, to name but a few.

Whatever Kluski was doing, it seemed that he was tapping into great monster-motifs. Some current, some ancient, and some yet to flourish. Dragons were noticeably absent, but Kluski's séances were held indoors, with hardly room for a dragon to manifest. One wonders what would have happened if he had tried an outdoor session – perhaps beside a lake?

While searching for the giant semi-aquatic snake – the naga – in Thailand, I noticed some of the great archetypes once again. In Thai mythology there are three main monsters:

> The naga – a water-dwelling serpent.
>
> The garuda – a creature, half-man, half-bird who is believed to bring the rains on his wings.
>
> The singa – a giant golden lion.

These creatures are said to inhabit a mystic jungle. Perhaps the 'mystic jungle' is the tangled reaches of our subconscious. Maybe Kluski was unconsciously manifesting the fears of the collective mind of the human race. This may sound absurd but there is evidence that such a thing actually exists.

British biologist Rupert Sheldrake infuriated adherents to academic dogma in 1981 when he published his revolutionary theories in a book entitled *A New Science of Life*. In this book Sheldrake raised the question of how – if every DNA molecule contained the coded information to make a specific creature – did the body know just what went where. For example, how did it know to grow skin-cells, and not say muscle-cells in the right areas. Also, many animals (like some lizards), can re-grow lost-limbs, while others – such as echinoderms – can be totally destroyed, (for example by putting them in a liquidiser), but each piece will re-grow into a fully-formed adult.

Sheldrake realised that contained within the DNA must be something akin to a 'blueprint' for each species – a life-shaping field unique to each life-form that orders the DNA. He called his hypothetical blueprints 'morphogenic fields' – or 'm-fields' for short. The m-field theory might also explain how subjective information like emotions and memories are retained. The cells in our bodies are constantly dying and being replaced, and this includes brain tissue. Yet we retain our memories and personalities – except under conditions of severe or maximum brain damage (even minimal to moderate brain-damage is self-repairable) – *ergo* something must be making the new molecules follow the exact patterns of their forbears.

This m-field template may be the key to understanding other biological mysteries such as migration. Darwin believed that this kind of information was passed on in the genetic-characteristics of the parents, but some startling experiments have challenged this view.

In the USA a series of experiments were carried out on rats. The rats had to learn how to escape from a pool of water without following the most logical course – as this had been rigged to give them an electric shock. The first generation took a number of attempts to learn this. The young of these rats took less time to work out the problem. This seemed to be supporting the Darwinian idea, but identical experiments were being carried out in another country with rats that had no genetic relationship to the ones in America. These rats took even less time to solve the puzzle than the second generation of rats in the American labs.

Sheldrake believed that this was because of a shared m-field. He hypothesised the m-fields of all individuals of a species were linked to a huge gestalt m-field. He proposed that evolutionary changes, behavioural patterns and information were shared at a subconscious level between the whole species. When individuals pick up advantageous new behavioural traits, it is incorporated into the gestalt. He believed this was passed on by resonance, rather like the way that the energy wave from a plucked string on an instrument can resonate onto another string on the same instrument that has not been plucked. This works because part of the unplucked string has the potential to resonate at frequencies in common with the vibrating string and thus can resonate in harmony. In music this is called harmonic resonance. Sheldrake called his biological analogue, morphic resonance.

Of course the inverse of this also occurred, wherein the individual's behaviour is altered by the m-field of the species. Animals with fewer turnovers of generations – those with longer life spans – would have m-fields that work more slowly. But they work nonetheless. Some Einstein of the sheep-world worked out how to cross cattle grids in Britain. The sheep curled up in a ball, and rolled across the grid! Initially only a few did this trick, but within weeks sheep all over the world were making POW-style escapes from farms.

This would seem to be the ideal was for gigantic 'racial thought forms' to occur. Perhaps we should seek the origin of dragons and other monsters, in the jungles of our own minds, and in the fossil memories handed down to us in our genes from our remote ancestors.

Several million years ago, on the plains of East Africa, our remote ancestors were struggling to survive. *Australopithecus* had an existence fraught with peril. In moving down from the trees, and onto the grassland to exploit untapped food-sources, he faced new and deadly enemies. The crocodile was – and is – the biggest natural killer of mankind. The rock-python would also have found our ancestors easy prey. *Australopithecus* was small enough to have fallen victim to large raptors, and fossil evidence from South Africa supports this. Lions and leopards would have certainly preyed on our ancestors, and hunting dogs may have also given them sleepless nights. *Australopithecus* and its descendants would have been in direct competition with other primate species. Some were smaller than itself – others, including the horrific giant baboon *Dinopithecus* – were larger.

Think about it. Here we have the genesis of mankind's monsters, the beginning of our species' bugbears. The dragon, the giant bird, the mystery big-cat, the phantom dog, the little people and the hairy giant.

Sheldrake himself seems to support this notion:

> 'In the early stages of a form's history, the morphogenetic field will be relatively ill-defined and significantly influenced by individual variants. But as time goes on, the cumulative influence of countless

previous systems will confer an ever-increasing
stability on the field; the more probable the average
type becomes, the more likely that it will be repeated
in the future.'

Perhaps our fossil memories can be triggered by certain things in our surroundings. Maybe some kinds of electromagnetic-interference coupled with the right person, with the right brain chemistry, in the right place, at the right time, can create a monster. If the brain – an electro-chemical computer – is 'shorted' it 're-boots' like an mechanical computer, and for a while switches to its most primitive 'operating-system'. In this condition, our m-field kicks in, and together with our fossil-memories, creates a defence mechanism – the primal fear, 'flight or fight', taken to its extreme in the creation of something visible and (for a time, at least) tangible.

There is, however, another possibility about the nature of dragons – a disquieting one. Namely that they are truly real creatures, not products of our minds but fully independent and living in another dimension.

The idea of other realities that co-exist with ours is not new. In the Middle Ages this place was called 'fairyland'. In the Victorian era it was known as the 'astral plane'. Modern writers have many names for it, John Keel calls it the 'super-spectrum', Jerry Clark the 'outer-edge' and F.W. Holliday the 'goblin-universe'. This elsewhere is the postulated domain of just about every monster, phantom and weird entity ever reported.

Perhaps this hypothetical dimension is separated from our own world by speed. We know that atoms oscillate at a certain frequency. Is it possible then, that other realities are composed of atoms that oscillate at different rates, either faster or slower than the norm? Such atoms could conceivably co-exist in the same space as the atoms in our dimension. Normally the objects made from these other atoms would be invisible to the naked eye. Perhaps these atoms can occasionally speed up/slow down for a time, and hence the things they compose become visible to us. Modern physics is now becoming like age-old magic with physicists postulating between six and eleven dimensions!

In Islamic lore there is a race of daemons known as *djinn*. This is where the Western concept of the genie is derived from. Djinn were not one type of creature but came in as many kinds as there are animals in our dimension. The Koran devotes a whole chapter to them. They are said to inhabit our world, but are usually invisible to us and we to them. Sometimes the veil slips and the djinn are seen.

A Muslim friend of mine, Mohamed Bula, related several stories he had heard of djinn in India. One was seen sitting beneath a rosebush. It grew from a tiny baby to an old man in seconds and then returned to its child form and repeated the process. Another witness reported that he had slipped through to the djinn's reality, and could see hundreds of robed figures apparently attending the funeral of one of their peers. Finally one man reported encountering a djinn on a remote beach. He saw a trail of footprints apparently stopping with no one to make them. Looking back he saw a figure walking away in the distance and knew it was a djinn – for their feet are supposed to point backwards. This last point may seem odd but it recurs all over the world in many different supernatural creatures. The Brazilian curupira is a hairy forest spirit, which is also said to possess these preposterous paws, as are some of the phantom black dogs.

This slipping in and out of realities is also a common feature of Fortean events The djinn stories are clearly indicative of this. Indian dragons are called nagas and seen as spirit creatures rather than flesh and blood.

Jerome Clark and D. Scott Rogo point out an interesting factor of monster sightings in their book *Earth's Secret Inhabitants*. They note that most reported monsters resemble real animals either living or extinct.

> 'Odd caricatures of the types of life-forms that
> populate the earth…these creatures represent the
> outcome of some evolutionary process paralleling life
> on this planet, but not exactly corresponding to it.'

In other words, the monsters come not from some other sphere, but a parallel reality within our own.

In this chapter I have been looking at the nature of that nebulous word we called 'reality'. Way back in 1748 David Hume, in his book *An Enquiry Concerning Human Understanding*, wrote that no amount of evidence could prove the reality of an event that violated the laws of nature as it was more likely that the evidence was wrong than a law of nature had been overturned. Yet these are the laws of humans, not the laws of nature. Humanity is fond of erecting false barriers and squeezing things into boxes. Perhaps it stems from a deep-seated fear of nature and a need to control it. Nature however will not be so tamed.

What we have been discussing will, I think, show just how fluid reality can be. Sheldrake has given us convincing evidence of a gestalt species mind, in other words, a field of shared subconscious – one that may well be inhabited by ancient terror in the manner tigers stalk through a jungle.

Kluski, David-Neel, and others have pointed to the way in which reality can be effected by the human mind, an idea that has recently resurfaced in modern physics with the idea that the act of simply observing particles effects them. Modern physicists might just as well be wizards, with their talk of multiple dimensions and the fleeting existence of particles.

Perhaps these are all just modern terms for that force our ancestors called 'magic'. In the twentieth century wizards have evoked dragons and priests have attempted to exorcise them. Cast aside the modern trappings and you could be looking at a centuries-old folktale.

Dragons inhabited the depths of the sea and the heights of the sky. The dragon still manifests today, but perhaps its true domains are the depths of our minds, and the heights of the 'super-spectrum'.

Chapter Seven
Sightings of dragons in the modern age

Like nightmares come to life, dragons are not content with living only in storybooks. Astounding, as it may seem dragon-like creatures are still reported today from all over the globe. It is not only remote mountains and jungles that these reports come from; sometimes they are much closer to home. In this chapter we will look at sightings of British dragons from the age of reason.

Dragons on the wing

A colony of small gaudily-coloured dragons was supposed to have nested close to Penllyn Castle, Glamorgan, Wales, early in the nineteenth century and some were even shot! These incredible events were uncovered by folklorist Marie Trevelyan while researching her book *Folk and Folk Stories of Wales*.

The woods around Penllyn Castle had a reputation for being frequented by winged serpents, and these were the terror of young and old alike. A detailed description of these fantastic beasts was given to Trevelyan by an aged inhabitant of Penllyne who died around 1900. He said that in his boyhood the winged serpents were described as very beautiful. They were coiled when in repose, and 'looked as if they were covered with jewels of all sorts. Some of them had crests sparkling with all the colours of the rainbow'. When disturbed, they glided swiftly, 'sparkling all over' to their hiding place. When angry, they 'flew over people's heads with outspread wings bright, and sometimes with eyes too, like the feathers of a peacock's tail.'

He said it was 'no old story invented to frighten children,' but a real fact. His father and uncle had killed some of them, for they were 'as bad as foxes for poultry.' The old man attributed the extinction of the winged serpents to the fact that they were 'terrors in farmyards and coverts.'

Unlike some other dragon manifestations these creatures seem flesh and blood. Indeed many were said to have been shot. Indeed they may well have, like so many other 'inconvenient' creatures, which suffered extinction at mankind's brutal hand. We see this in the next account and also the association between dragons and buried treasure. This link, like the storms mentioned above seems to be widespread in dragon lore.

An old woman, whose parents in her early childhood took her to visit Penmark Place, Glamorgan, said she often heard the people talking about the ravages of the winged serpents in that neighbourhood. She described them in the same way as the man of Penllyne. There was a 'king and queen' of the winged serpents, she said, in the woods around Bewper. The old people in the early days said that wherever winged serpents were seen 'there was sure to be buried money or something of value' near at hand. Her grandfather told her of an encounter with a winged serpent in the woods near Porthkerry Park, not far from Penmark. He and his brother made up their minds to catch one, and watched the whole day for the serpent to rise. Then they shot at it, and the creature fell wounded, only to rise and attack my uncle, beating him around the head with its wings.' She said a fierce fight ensued between the men and the serpent, which was at last killed. She had seen its skin and feathers, but after the grandfather's death they were thrown away. The serpent was as notorious 'as any fox' in the farmyards and coverts around Penmark.

It is truly frustrating that this priceless skin was discarded – it could well have been the most important zoological specimen of all time! This said, the very fact it was thrown out shows that the populace did not consider the winged serpents anything out of the ordinary. True, they were pretty, but also a pest to farmers and looked on in the same way as a fox or buzzard. It has been theorised that the serpents were some kind of tropical birds set free from captivity, but no birds that could prey on farm stock remotely resemble these Welsh wonders. Perhaps in some cellar or stock room of a museum, or in the attic of an old Welsh farm, some remains of these remarkable beasts still lie in wait for an incredulous scientific community to discover them.

In September 1982 a freakish animal was appearing in the skies above the Aire Valley in West Yorkshire. It was first spotted in a wooded area known as the Devil's Punchbowl on the 12th September. It flew low and erratically, on large, bat-like wings and, according to the anonymous witness, resembled a pterodactyl. The witness was interviewed by my friend and expert on the occult history of Ilkley Moor, Paul Bennett. It was also seen by a resident of nearby Eldwick, who described it as being grey with a pointed beak and short legs.

It returned on the night of the 15th, and was spotted by a man walking his dog in Pudsey. On hearing a loud scream, followed by a low groan, the man – fearing a mugging was taking place – investigated. The sounds were repeated from rooftop level, and he looked up to see a bat-winged, bird-like creature perched upon a neighbour's roof and towering over the chimney pots. He said:

> 'It was making a screaming call with its beak open,
> then grunt with its beak closed. It launched itself from
> the roof, its weight causing it to drop below roof
> level, before its slow wing beat carried it off into the
> darkness.'

The witness estimated the monster's wingspan to be eight feet (three metres). It was seen again in Yeadon, flying towards the airport. Then the sightings trailed off until 7th June the following year. A woman living in Thackley, Bradford, saw it flying with laborious strokes down her street towards a wooded, disused railway. The massive size astonished her.

Mike Priestly, features editor on the *Telegraph and Argus* and twice 'Yorkshire Reporter of The Year' decided to track the mystery down and photograph it. His patience was rewarded when he snapped a large flying creature in the skies above Bradford. His 300mm telephoto lens was unable to get a clear picture because of the extreme distance of the subject. The thing in Priestly's photograph however is clearly a bird and not a reptile. Perhaps he captured a large bird of prey such as a buzzard on film.

Reports of the beast continued from Baildon, Shipley, Crossflats, Pudsey, Yeadon and Thackley. The last recorded sighting occurred in November 1985. Journalist Malcolm Hodds described a black beast with a 1.5 metre wingspan and finger-like feathers.

The Yorkshire pterodactyl flap was over, but on the other side of the Pennines a remarkably similar monster reared its head in 1999. Ian Wharton told me of the strange encounters of two of his colleagues in the Parks Department working at Hesketh Park, Southport. One man, Clive Everson, approached Wharton one morning in having claimed to have just seen what looked like a pterodactyl. A grey skinned, bat-winged creature, with a long beak and massive wingspan, had risen up out of the bushes in front of Everson, and flown away leaving him dazed and alarmed.

A second man, Percy Whaterton, had seen two beasts answering the same description in the woods that backed onto his house. These strange creatures were badly frightening the birds in the park and Whaterton thought that they may be nesting in the forest. To date nothing further has been heard from this area.

Further north, winged dragons have made their presence felt. Damien Smith and his two uncles were walking one evening in the north-west Highlands of Scotland. They were in a remote part of Sutherland and stopping in a cabin. The surrounding area was uninhabited and consisted of miles of bleak, open moorland. The nearest town was 50 kilometres away. It was 10.30 at night and the men were returning to the cabin. As they walked up the driveway they all heard a flapping sound. Their torches revealed a huge flying creature with a wingspan of between twelve and twenty feet (4 to 6.5 metres). It had a long beak and was grey in colour. They were certain that it was not a heron or eagle, both of which they had seen many times before.

In 1996, Neil Mitchelson was camping in the Lake District, between Little Longdale and Coniston. There was a full moon and he and his friends had a large fire burning. He noticed a shape beneath the clouds, moving left to right. As it drew closer he alerted his companions, and all ten campers watched a manta ray-shaped object, with a 11 metre wingspan flying in the night sky. They could clearly see the wings flapping.

In the late 1990s I received several anonymous phone call claiming that a dragon-like creature had returned to the skies above Ilkley. The caller said a black-skinned, leathery-winged creature the size of a helicopter had been seen on several occasions. I could not verify the story so make of it what you will.

Dragons in lochs and lakes

We most often associate the dragon with the element of fire. World-wide it is more closely linked with water. In China and Japan dragons were said to have control of water causing floods or droughts if angered but also bringing life-giving rains with their breath. In Sumaria and Babylon the most ancient of known civilisations the dragon is a beast of the water. Therefore we should not be too surprised that most modern encounters with dragon-like creatures take place in this element.

Gouged out by glaciers in the Ice Age, Loch Ness runs like a livid scar across the Great Glen of Scotland. Twenty-three miles long, a

The Loch Ness Monster from an old postcard. The unknown artist chose to depict an amphibious creature capable of moving fast enough over land to be able to successfully hunt local lambs.

mile wide, and over 800 feet (258 metres) deep, the loch is a fitting abode for a dragon. It is said that the entire population of the world – every man, woman, and child – could fit into the loch three times over, and still there would be room for more. The waters are stained inky black by masses of peat washed down from the surrounding hills. This reduces underwater visibility to only a few feet. The cool temperature (42 Celsius) and treacherous undercurrents add to the loch's dark reputation.

Legends of something odd in the waters date back to at least AD 565 when the oft-repeated story of St Columba was said to have occurred. The Irish saint was in Scotland converting the Picts to Christianity, when he met a water monster said to have bitten a man to death in the River Ness (not the loch). He overcame the brute with his holy powers and since then, according to legend, it has been harmless.

In mediaeval times the creatures were known as water horses or kelpies, and were believed to drag down and devour humans. It seems that St Columba had as little luck in exorcising the monster as Donald Ormand did centuries later. Many locals saw some massive creature in the waters over the years, but few reports travelled far. All this aside, the monster did not achieve true fame in the outside world until 1933 – shortly after a lochside road had been built, making the remote area more accessible. A young couple – called the Mackays – were motoring along the northern shore, when they saw a churning of the water, and observed the two humped back of a huge animal disporting itself in the water. Shortly afterwards, the *Inverness Courier* dubbed it a monster, and the phrase 'Loch Ness Monster' was born.

From then until now the monster has had more written about it than any other mystery creature. Enough volumes to fill a library have been penned on the subject, and the Loch Ness Monster is now surely the most famous monster in the world. An Identikit picture from witness descriptions creates a large-bodied animal with a long neck terminating in a small head, a somewhat shorter tail and four turtle-like flippers. The average length seems to be nine to twelve metres and the colour an 'elephant' grey. I will not spend time and space repeating sightings that have been discussed *ad nauseam* elsewhere although there are several eyewitness accounts in Chapter Five. Instead I will look at the less well-known lake monsters that inhabit our country.

Most people wrongly assume that Loch Ness is the world's only monster-haunted lake. They could not be more wrong. Many lakes in many countries have reports of anomalous animals attached to them. In fact in Scotland alone there are around 34 such bodies of water. After Loch Ness, Loch Morar is the most famous. Morar is a deep glacial loch much like Loch Ness. At eleven miles long it is smaller, but its depth of 1,000 feet (323 metres) makes it the deepest lake in the UK. Its resident monsters have been named 'Morag' – a derivative of the Gaelic *mordhobhar* meaning 'big water'. In centuries past it was believed that Morag would only show itself if a member of a certain Scottish clan was about to die. Morag could appear as a fair maiden or a great serpent.

So much for folklore, but in the age of enlightenment may people claim to have seen a monstrous creature in Loch Morar. In fact the Loch is second only to Loch Ness in reported sightings. Sightings like that of John MacVarish barman at the Morar Hotel on 27th August 1968:

> 'I saw this thing coming. I thought it was a man
> standing in a boat but as it got nearer I saw it was
> something coming out of the water. I tried to get up
> close to it with the outboard out of the water and
> what I saw was a long neck five or six feet out of the
> water with a small head on it, dark in colour, coming

quite slowly down the loch. When I got to about 300 yards of it, it turned off into the deep and just settled down slowly into the loch out of sight.

The neck was about one and a half feet in diameter, and tapered up to between ten inches and a foot. I never saw any features, no eyes or anything like that. It was a snake like head, very small compared to the size of the neck – flattish, a flat type of head. It seemed to have very smooth skin, but at 300 yards its difficult to tell. It was very dark, nearly black.

It was 10 a.m., dead calm, no wind, brilliant sunshine. I saw it for about ten minutes travelling very slowly: it didn't alter its angle to the water. It looked as if it was paddling itself along. There was very little movement from the water, just a small streak from the neck. I couldn't really see what was propelling it but I think it was something at the sides rather than behind it.'

Earlier the same year, Robert Duff got a clearer look at the creature. Duff, a joiner from Edinburgh, was fishing in Meoble Bay on the Loch's south shore. It was 8th July. The water was about five metres deep and very clear. The bottom was pale, almost white with leaves on it. Lying on the bottom was what Duff described as a giant lizard over six metres long. The skin was a dirty brown colour, and he saw three digits on the beast's front limbs. It was motionless and looking up at him with slit-like eyes. Terrified he revved up his motorboat and made his escape.

The most dramatic encounter took place on 16th August 1969. Duncan McDonnell and William Simpson were returning from a trip up the loch. It was around 9.00 p.m. but still light. McDonnell was at the wheel and the boat was doing seven knots. He writes:

I heard a splash or disturbance in the water astern of us. I looked up and saw about twenty yards behind us this creature coming directly after us in our wake. It only took a matter of seconds to catch up with us. It grazed the side of the boat, I am quite certain this was unintentional. When it struck the boat seemed to come to a halt or at least slow down. I grabbed the oar and was attempting to fend it off, my one fear being that if it got under the boat it might capsize it.

Simpson wrote...

> 'As we were sailing down the loch in my boat, we
> were suddenly disturbed and frightened by a thing
> that surfaced behind us. We watched it catch us up
> then bump into the side of the boat, the impact sent a
> kettle of water I was heating onto the floor. I ran into
> the cabin to turn the gas off as the water had put the
> flame out. Then I came out of the cabin to see my
> mate trying to fend the beast off with an oar, to me
> he was wasting his time. Then when I seen the oar
> break I grabbed my rifle and quickly putting a bullet
> in it fired in the direction of the beast. Then I
> watched it slowly sink away from the boat and that
> was the last I seed of it'.

Neither of the men seemed to think that the bullet had any effect on
the monster. They estimated it to be nine metres long. The skin was
rough and dirty-brown in colour. It had three humps that protruded
half a metre out of the water. McDonnell thought they may have
been undulations rather than humps. McDonnell reported seeing a
snake-like head, thirty centimetres across, held half a metre out of
the water.

I spent several days trying to bait out the monster of Loch Morar in
April 2000. I used hessian sacks full of meat and chemical
attractants. These were suspended via floats. The bait remained
untouched but I learnt of a totally unrecorded recent sighting. While
stopping at the delightful Garremore House bed and breakfast my
host, Julia Moore, told me that about three years previously two
young men from Yorkshire had come to the loch on a fishing trip.
They camped by the shore and rented a boat. As they were going
across the loch the lad on lookout shouted to his mate, who was
operating the tiller, that a tree trunk was approaching the boat. Both
of them saw what looked like a big log in the water. To their horror
they realised that it was moving against the waves and heading
towards them. It was in fact some huge, elongated creature. Just as
they thought a collision was imminent it arched up in the water and
dove beneath them. They rowed to shore like Oxford's finest,
packed up and went straight back home.

Loch Shiel is seventeen miles long, a mile wide and 420 feet (135
metres) deep. Its monster has been unsurprisingly named 'Sheila'.

Father Cyril Dieckhoff of the Benedictine Abbey at Fort Augustus collected many accounts of the creature and was planning to write a book. Sadly he died in 1970 leaving his work unpublished. One of the earliest reports is from 1905. An old man called Ian Crookback and two boys watched through a telescope at a three-humped creature as they crossed the loch opposite Gasgan in a mail steamer.

Another report is of a long-necked monster with a wide mouth and seven humps. It was observed through a telescope by Ronald McLeod as it emerged from the water near Sandy Point in 1926.

Loch Oich lies directly below Loch Ness. In 1936 a headmaster and member of the Camberwell Borough Council, his son, and two friends, saw the loch's monster while boating in fairly shallow water. Two humps like the coils of a snake emerged only a few metres from the boat. The coils were a metre long, a metre high, and a metre apart from each other. Then a dog-like head emerged. They watched the creature rise and dive several times.

Loch Lochy lies below Loch Oich and is Scotland's third deepest after Morar and Ness. On 30th September 1975 at 2.00 p.m. Mr and Mrs Sargent and their two children were driving along the south shore road. As they turned the corner by the Corriegour hotel they saw a six metre black hump gliding through the water, creating a wave. Mr Sargent slowed his van and his wife fumbled with her camera as the great wash hit the shore. Sadly the hump submerged before she could get a shot. Meanwhile, Mr Sargent stopped the van further up the road, and saw a smaller hump following the first. Mrs Sargent did not notice this second hump. The whole sighting lasted about two minutes. Mrs Sargent noticed his wife was visibly shaking, and that the children were shouting excitedly.

In 1996 a 3.6 metre dark-coloured animal was seen swimming in the loch. It had a curved head and three humps. The creature swam in circles while being observed by staff and guests at the Corriegour hotel. One witness – Catronia Allen, an Aberdeen University psychology student – observed it through binoculars and said that it was not an otter, dolphin, porpoise or seal.

The following year, a six-man expedition including Loch Ness witness and researcher Garry Campbell, and diver Cameron Turner, conducted a sonar sweep of Loch Lochy. Near the centre of the loch they picked up an unidentified reading indicating a six metre object swimming in the water.

Loch Treig lies beneath Britain's tallest mountain, Ben Nevis. Back in 1933 a hydro-electric scheme was started in the Loch. B.N. Peach, the man in charge of the scheme, reported that many divers left their jobs after encountering monsters underwater. Sadly little more detail on this case is available.

At Easter 1980, Mr and Mrs Maltman and their daughter were camping at Loch Lomond. They were terrified to see a five-foot long head and neck with a bulky body behind it, rear up from the water nearly 300 metres from were they sat. The beast was visible for thirty seconds. The Maltmans were so scared that they fled, leaving their belongings at the loch-side.

If few people have heard of lake monsters other than Nessie in Scotland, fewer still can have heard of the strange creatures sighted in Welsh lakes.

Llyn y Gadair is a small round lake near to Snowdon. In the eighteenth century a man decided to swim across it. His friends who were waiting for him on the bank were horrified to see a long trailing object winding after him. As he approached the shore it reared up and seized him. Winding about him like a python, it dragged him down into the lake.

At Glaslyn, another lake in the Snowdon range, a monster was spotted in the 1930s. Two climbers looking down on the lake saw a long grey body with a pale head rise to the surface then dive again. It was unlike any other creature either of them had seen before.

But it is Llyn Tegid (or Lake Bala) that has gained the most fame. At four miles long and 150 feet (nearly 50 metres) deep Lake Bala is a puddle compared to Loch Ness. It lies in Gwynedd in north Wales. Legend has it that the lake was created by a water spirit who dwelt in a well. He provided water for the surrounding villages. One night a local man forgot to replace the wooden boards that cover the well every evening. In the morning the people awoke to see a lake.

Mrs Ann Jones saw the now-familiar hump aspect moving across the lake in October 1979. Mr John Melville was fishing on the lake with cousin in the same year and got a more detailed look.

> 'It had a large head, like a football and rather big
> eyes. We could see the body which was 8 feet long.
> It wasn't aggressive at all. It swam to within a few
> yards of us then turned and disappeared. I wouldn't

say I had seen a monster, just a large being. But I
have caught some rather big pike in the lake before
now and it was bigger than any of those.'

In March 1995 Paul and Andrew Delaney from London were fishing
on the lake, when they noticed something about eighty metres from
their boat. The brothers initially thought it was a tree trunk until it
rose up three metres out of the water. It was an elongated neck with
a small head. The brothers said it reminded them of pictures of the
Loch Ness monster.

Veteran Australian cryptozoologist and author of the excellent book
Out of the Shadows; the Mystery animals of Australia, Tony Healy
told me of his trip to Lake Bala in the 1980s. He interviewed two
men who had been out fishing on a boat. Something that resembled
the back of a cow – large, rounded and brown – surfaced close to
their boat. The men were so frightened that they never went back
onto the lake.

So what are the strange creatures living in these lakes? Theories
have included long-necked seals, giant otters, huge amphibians and
even prehistoric invertebrates. The most popular theory is that
Nessie is a surviving form of plesiosaur or something descended
from them. These were long-necked sea-dwelling aquatic reptiles of
the mid- to late-Mesozoic era. Loch Ness with its fresh water, cold
temperature and poor fish stocks could not be a much more
inhospitable place for them.

If air-breathing animals were behind the lake monster riddle, then
they would be seen at the surface more often. The sonar readings
suggest the creatures are benthic or bottom dwelling, and that they
derive their oxygen directly from the water. Some sort of fish would
seem the obvious choice. A titanic eel would seem the best
candidate. With its sinuous form it can rear up to resemble a long
neck and head. Though they flex themselves in the horizontal plane,
eels can swim at the surface on their sides, and resemble a series of
humps moving in the vertical plane. Therefore a stout-bodied eel in
the six to nine metre range would make a very fitting lake monster
or worm for that matter.

Eels have a curious breeding cycle. Mature eels swim out of their
fresh water homes and into the Atlantic when they are ready to
breed. Amazingly they follow scent trails hundreds of miles across
the ocean to the Sargasso Sea off Florida were they breed then die.

The young eels or leptocephalus follow the trails back to the freshwater abodes of their ancestors where they mature for a number of years before the cycle begins again.

Occasionally the cycle is broken for some individuals. These never develop sexually and so do not leave fresh water to breed. They stay sedentary and continue to grow. Known as eunuch eels, these fish are reputed to reach a great age and size. A specimen was reported from the Birmingham Ship Canal in the 1980s that was 6.5 metres long. Another the same size was reputedly caught in the cooling system of an aluminium works at Dores on the shore of Loch Ness. A eight metre eel was observed in the shallows of Loch Ness by some Canadian tourists in February 2004. They were walking along a beach when they saw the creature almost grounded in the shallows. Thinking it was dead they approached. When it began to wriggle they led in terror. They describe it as grey and looking like an anaconda.

We must not forget the odder aspects of the Loch that we examined in the previous chapter on esoteric theories. A good Fortean keeps an open mind. Many monster sightings have very weird aspects and may be something more complex than an unknown animal. These bodies of water may be the home to gigantic eels and dragon-like beasts of a more nebulous character.

Dragons in the sea

If lakes can hold strange creatures then what about the sea? Even the largest loch is but a drop of water in comparison. The sea is the ancestral home of the dragon. Tiamat the Babylonian dragon goddess resided there, as did the world-encircling Jormungander or Midguard Serpent in Norse legend. Sea dragons come in a variety of shapes and sizes and are no strangers to British waters.

The many-humped sea serpent is an animal with a fairly short neck, a long body and either a row of humps on the back or a flexible spine that loops up in coils out of the water. It undulates vertically.

Mr George Ashton, a 49-year old shot-blaster from Sheffield, and his wife May saw such a beast a hundred metres from shore at Chapel St Leonards in October 1966.

> 'It had a head like a serpent, and six or seven pointed
> humps trailing behind. When I have been out at sea, I
> have seen seal and sea snakes swimming about and
> what I saw was neither of these. At first I thought it

was a log but it was travelling at about 8 m.p.h. and going parallel with the shore. We watched it for some time, coming from the direction of Chapel Point, until it disappeared out of sight towards Ingoldmells. I just didn't believe in these things and tried to convince myself it was a flight of birds just above the water. I even thought of a miniature submarine, but after watching it for sometime, I knew it couldn't be.'

If the word of a shot-blaster isn't good enough for you, then how about the daughter of one of our country's greatest novelists? On 20th July 1912 Miss Lilias Haggard, daughter of Sir Henry Rider Haggard, was privy to a sighting that could have slithered from the pages of one of her father's novels. She wrote to him from her home, Kessingland Grange, East Anglia, to tell him of the encounter:

'We had great excitement here this evening. And we are convinced we saw a sea serpent! I happened to look up when I was sitting on the lawn, and saw what looked like a thin, dark line with a blob at one end, shooting through the water at such a terrific speed it hardly seemed likely that anything alive could go at such a pace. It was some way out over the sandbank, and travelling parallel with the shore. I tore into the morning room and got the glasses, and though it had, at that moment nearly vanished in the distance, we could make out it had a sort of head at one end and then a series of about 30 pointed blobs, which dwindled in size as they neared the tail. As it went along it seemed to get more and more submerged, and then vanished. You can't imagine the pace it was going. I suppose it was about 60 feet long.'

Her father sent the letter to the *Eastern Daily Press* along with a letter from himself asking if anyone else had seen the creature. A number of people responded. Mr C.G. Harding said that he has seen saw a long, dark creature moving through the water like a torpedo the day after Miss Haggard's sighting. Mrs Adelaide J. Orams and her son had seen a dark object swimming out to sea at Mundesley. An anonymous woman claimed to have seen it three weeks previously, moving with 'lightning rapidity' opposite the harbour mouth at Gorleston. Mr W.H. Sparow and his wife had seen it the day before the Haggard sighting from the promenade at Cromer. It was moving at 40 m.p.h. and undulating. He estimated it to be nine metres long.

These long-necked creatures are one of the commonest reported sea-serpent types. They bear a superficial resemblance to a plesiosaur but this may be due to parallel evolution. They may well be reptilian as many reports speak of a long tail, a feature not seen in large marine mammals.

The long-necked sea serpent – as its name suggests – has a snaky, elongated neck. Its body is shorter than the many-humped but considerably wider. The animal has two sets of flippers attached to the barrel-shaped body, as well as a tail at the rear. Some confusion may arise between the many-humped and the long-necked. The body of the long-necked can show up to five humps, but never as many as the many-humped. The humps of the long-necked seem to be flexations in the back or possibly fat storage as in camels. The humps of the many-humped would appear to be the loops of its elongated body showing as it propels itself. When rearing up with the front portion of the body, the many-humped can seem to have a long neck. The long-necked however really does have a long neck, quite separate from the bulbous body. Sometimes a dorsal fin is reported on the back of the long necked, but these reports are in the minority.

The largest concentration of sightings have been around Cornwall where the monster is known as 'Morgawr' (which allegedly means 'sea giant' in archaic Cornish). Harold T. Wilkins and a friend saw two specimens while at the shark fishing port of Looe in 1949.

Two remarkable saurians about six metres long with bottle-green heads, one behind the other, their middle parts under the water of the tidal creek of Looe, east Cornwall, were apparently chasing a shoal of fish up the creek. What was amazing were their dorsal parts: rigid, serrated and like the old Chinese pictures of dragons. Gulls swooped down towards the rear of one. These monsters – two of which were seen –resembled the plesiosaurus of Mesozoic times.

Twenty-six years later, the *Falmouth Packet* newspaper reported the first in a whole series of modern sightings. Two witnesses, Mrs Scott and Mr Riley, had seen the thing off Pendennis Point. They described a long neck and a small head furnished with stubby horns. The neck had what looked like a mane of bristles running along it. The monster dived, and surfaced holding a large conger eel in its mouth. Mrs Scott commented that she would never forget the face on the thing as long as she lived.

On the 28th of December 1975 Mr Gerald Bennett wrote to the same paper about his own sighting.

> 'I myself, during the last Christmas holidays, witnessed the sighting of a similar creature (to that seen by Mrs Scott and Mr Riley), although until now I have remained reticent about it. It was off the shore at Durgan, Helford, about 4 p.m., near dusk. When I first spotted it, I thought it was a dead whale, but as I drew nearer it started to move away, smoothly, and I could see it was not a whale, nor like any creature seen round here. I judged that the part of it I could see above water was about 12 feet in length with an elongated neck.'

In January 1976 Duncan Viner, a dental technician, saw a twelve metre monster off Rosemullion Head. He too thought it was a whale until a long neck emerged from the water.

Later the same month, Amelia Johnson saw it in the same area, and described it as 'A sort of prehistoric, dinosaur thing, with a long neck, which was the length of a lamppost.'

Soon after the *Falmouth Packet* received two photographs from a woman calling herself 'Mary F'. The appeared to show a large animal with a long neck on the surface of the water. Unfortunately there was little in the shots to give scale. In the accompanying letter 'Mary F' said she had seen the monster off Trefusis Point in early February. She claimed to have been badly frightened by the animal. She had sold the negatives, or so she said, to 'an American gentleman'.

It has since been suggested that the 'Mary F' pictures were fakes made using modelling clay on sheets of glass. It has also been suggested that the culprit was the late John Gordon, a friend of Doc Sheils. The faked photographs of 'Shiela' – the so-called Loch Shiel monster which appear in *The Shiels Effect* a book about (and probably by) Shiels, are credited to a J.B. Gordon. The fact that the negatives or their American buyer have never surfaced, seems to reinforce the idea that they are fakes, even though the perpetrator cannot conclusively be named.

Sightings continued. Two London bankers, Tony Rodgers and John Chambers, were fishing on the rocks of Parson's Beach at the mouth of the Helford River, when they saw Morgawr. It was green-grey in colour and bore humps. Rodgers thought he saw a second smaller creature accompanying the first.

In the summer of 1976 George Vinnicombe and John Cock were fishing the wartime wrecks 25 miles out from Lizard Point. Once again, a dead whale was thought to be the object they saw floating on the calm surface. The idea was quashed as a serpentine head and neck rose up before the monster dived.

Brother and sister Allan and Sally Whyte came upon the monster on land. The brown coloured six metre animal was resting on Grebe beach and slithered into the sea at their approach.

The editor of *Cornish Life*, David Clarke joined Doc Sheils on one of his monster invocations on the rocks below Mawnan as Doc attempted to raise Morgawr from the Helford River on 17th November 1976. Clarke took shots of Doc's incantations beside the river, then to his amazement a rounded back and small head surfaced. Clarke noticed small horns on the greenish creature's head as it swam up and down the river in a zigzag pattern. Clarke took shots with a telephoto lens. Sadly the pictures were damaged by a triple exposure. However an odd-looking object can be seen lying low in the water.

More photos were taken in 1980 by Geoffrey Watson in the Mawnan area. He saw a pair of black humps rise up and move along the river from 300 metres away. He took a series of shots of the object as it swam away. Upon development the humps were too distant and indistinct to glean any useful information.

In July of 1985 two girls, Jenny Halstead and Alice Lee, from the lovely Yorkshire town of Hebden Bridge spotted the beast while on a cycling holiday.

'At some time between 6.30 and 7 pm, from a position at Rosemullion overlooking the sea, we witnessed a genuine living monster of the deep, which we believe must be your legendary monster Morgawr. The creature's back broke the surface and looked rather like a massive overgrown black slug. We both watched the animal for about ten seconds as it wallowed in the water. Then the creature sank beneath the waves and did not surface again. Even though we had a camera to hand, we were too astounded by the sight by the sight of the monster to think of taking a photograph until it was too late.'

Josh Tomkins, a fisherman, and his son were out in a boat a mile off Falmouth on 24th August 1999 at 4.30 p.m. when they saw something rise from the water.

'Initially I thought it was a dead body rising to the surface. As we watched the mound it dropped back under the water, causing a terrific swell. Moments later it resurfaced, about fifty yards from our boat. I could see that it was no dead body, but a large creature. My son thought it was the back of a whale as this was the most logical explanation we could find. Our opinions altered when, about ten yards in front of the mound, a small head appeared above the surface. The head lifted out of the water only very slightly but sufficient for both of us to see part of what seemed a long slender neck. It then dropped back down in a colossal disturbance.

We were both shocked by the immense size of the creature; it was like no fish I have ever seen, in fact it wasn't like anything I had seen before. I am pretty sure it must have been 'Morgawr' the sea monster. I didn't believe in this before and I am still not certain now, but that thing sure did look like a dinosaur-like creature. I would think it was dark brown or black, but the colouration was not evenly distributed, it seemed to be patchy in parts, slightly lighter in areas. We both saw its eyes, no ears and no mouth. It made no noise, just created a huge wash as it submerged. After seeing it, I would not be too happy about going out into open water after dark in a small boat; it's very large and could inflict some serious damage to a small vessel.'

Mrs Elsie Morgan saw it at around about the same time in the waters off Falmouth.

'I saw, about one hundred yards seaward a black object appear in the water. It appeared before my eyes and seemed to be stationary. I would estimate that it was about ten feet long and, at its highest point out of the water, about two feet. As I watched, something rose out of the water close to the 'hump-like' mound. It appeared to rise to an angle of 45 degrees, and looked a bit like the curved end of a question mark, but more angular. I then realised that this was either the tail or the head and neck of some large marine animal. This dipped in and out of the water several times, its highest point appeared to be moving from side to side, like the head of a snake looking around. It remained in sight for a minute or two before sinking from view. I could see white foam on the sea surface where it disappeared. It wasn't like any sort of animal or fish I had ever seen, nor could I imagine what it looked like as a whole, but it was very large and looked quite cumbersome.'

The most recent sighting to date occurred off Falmouth again on 16th May 2000. Derek and Irene Brown had parked their caravan overlooking the sea.

'The sea was quite calm, not choppy or heavily disturbed, and the weather was reasonably good, by that I mean that no mist or rain was falling and visibility was clear for a considerable distance out to sea. As we sat next to our caravan overlooking the sea, I saw something appear in the water perhaps 200 yards away, certainly no more. I took no notice of the object as the sea does throw up debris and bits of driftwood and I had no reason to concentrate on the object. I looked away and heard Irene ask me 'What is that out there?' I looked again as she pointed to the object I had glimpsed a few moments earlier. The object now took the form of defined humps, two of them very close together. I would think that overall they measured about 15 feet. I estimated that from my height, I am just over 6 feet tall. The humps were still, and as I sat searching for an explanation to give Irene, a periscope-like object came out of the water very close to these humps. It was moving in a flexible manner, not at all rigid. I would think it looked close to the stance a cobra or python makes, raising its head and neck before it strikes. Irene shouted, 'It's an octopus', but it clearly wasn't. I took the humps to be the back of a large body, the periscope-like object being the head and neck. I told Irene that I thought it was a monster and to get the camera from the car as we should take a picture of it.

As she got up to leave me, the creature seemed to roll forward, dipping head first into the water. There was a huge commotion as it disappeared. Irene came back with the camera but it had gone. We stayed to look for the creature for another hour, but it never resurfaced.

I cannot begin to explain how we felt about what we saw. We decided to keep it to ourselves, as no one would believe us and we would look stupid. I think the creature you are looking for is not one known to zoological science, but more to archaeologists who search for fossilized remains of creatures that existed many millions of years ago. This may sound stupid and far fetched, but somehow I believe that some of them lived on and exist in our waters. It wasn't a fish, more like a water based dinosaur, like something you see in those 1960 films about prehistoric times.

I am not a storyteller, not do I wish to capitalize upon what my wife and I saw, but I felt I should report this to someone, as it genuinely happened.'

Almost every county in Britain with a coastline has had reports of long-necked sea serpents. In August 1963 Mr P. Sharman was on holiday in Wales when he saw one from his vantage point on the cliffs. He was near New Quay, Cardigan Bay. He wrote to the late Tim Dinsdale with the details.

'I noticed an animal greatly disturbing a colony of seals. The creature drawn was slowly moving its four paddles two and fro as if in readiness to make a sudden move. At one end of it there appeared to be a long neck and small head poised above the water as if to strike out suddenly. The seals around it were making off as though the fear of death was upon them. This led me to suspect that the creature was making ready to kill a seal. After I had watched the thing for a few minutes I realised there was a remote possibility that I was looking down upon a floundering

169

basking shark. This seemed more and more probable, so I left the scene.

Later, during that week I was exploring another cove about half a mile from the spot were I saw the strange animal. Here I saw the carcass of a seal with a huge chunk bitten off from its neck and shoulders. This practically cut the body in two and I could not help wondering what creature could have made such a horrible wound. Of course it could be that I saw a basking shark half in and half out of the water and mistook the tail for the head and neck of a Plesiosaur type creature. But I saw no dorsal fin; and are basking sharks aggressive to seals? The creature, comparing it with the seals must have been 30–40 feet long, and was a brownish black in colour. I was looking down at it from about 100 feet at an angle of 50 degrees. It must have been 8 feet wide.'

Mr Sharman provided a drawing with his statement. It shows a large long-necked animal with a bulbous body, two pairs of flippers and a stout tail. All around, seals are scattering from it.

Filey Brig is a long, low spur of rocks jutting a mile out to sea from the coast of the Yorkshire seaside town of Filey. In local legend they are said to be the bones of a dragon. Fittingly it was here that one of the spookiest encounters with a long-necked sea serpent occurred. In February 1936 Wilkinson Herbert, a coastguard, was walking along the Brig on a dark, moonless night:

'Suddenly I heard a growling like a dozen dogs ahead, walking nearer I switched on my torch, and was confronted by a huge neck, six yards ahead of me, rearing up eight feet high!

The head was a startling sight, huge; tortoise eyes, like saucers, glaring at me, the creature's mouth was a foot wide and its neck would be a yard round.

The monster appeared as startled as I was. Shining my torch along the ground, I saw a body about 30 feet long. I though 'this is no place for me' and from a distance I threw stones at the creature. It moved away growling fiercely, and I saw the huge black body had two humps on it and four short legs with huge flappers on them. I could not see any tail. It moved quickly, rolling from side to side, and went into the sea. From the cliff top I looked down and saw two eyes like torch lights shining out to sea 300 yards away. It was a most gruesome and thrilling experience. I have seen big animals abroad but nothing like this.'

Further up the coast lies the county of Tyne and Wear. Nestled below South Shields is Marsden Bay; one of the strangest and most myth-ridden places in Britain. The small cove has an unearthly air about it, and it seems almost totally cut off from the rest of the world. One can easily forget the houses and shops a few hundred metres from the cliff tops. It is a tranquil, eerie place. Several hundred years ago an elderly man known as 'Blaster Jack' used blasting powder to blow himself a cave in the living rock. He and his wife used this as a home and later opened it up as a tavern. The tavern, known as Marsden Grotto, is still there today. From the time of Blaster Jack it was handed down from landlord to landlord. Parts of Lambton Castle, demolished in the eighteenth century are kept here, built into the Grotto's walls. On ancient pillar shows the infamous Lambton Wyrm, a huge serpent dragon that terrorised the area at the time of the crusades.

Local historian and Fortean researcher Mike Hallowell has unearthed a gruesome and almost unbelievable story concerning the area. According to his remarkable account during the Danelaw, when this part of England was ruled by the Norsemen, the Vikings were in dread of a sea dragon called the 'Shoney'. They placated the dragon with human sacrifice. The longship crews would draw straws. The loser would be bound hand and foot, have their throat slashed, and were tossed into the sea, in the hope that the Shoney would eat the man and not attack the ship. Bodies would wash up all along the coast from Lindisfarne to Marsden Bay. Sometimes they were virtually untouched, and other times they were half-eaten.

This practice became a sort of veneration, and was carried on by Scandinavian sailors long after the time of the Vikings as a dragon worship cult. Bodies that washed ashore in Marsden Bay were taken to the Grotto. The cellar was used as a kind of morgue on many occasions. Mike has been told that the last body was found in 1928!

If true this means that a dragon worship cult was practising human sacrifice in England well into the twentieth century. The story sounds like the script for a Hammer horror movie. Together with

David Curtis – a Fortean researcher from Seaham on Sea, Co. Durham – Mike is currently trying to gain access to police records for the period to try and verify this disturbing story. The investigation is currently being hampered by the fact that county boundaries have been changed on several occasions, and no one seems to know which police force has the records for the period. More worryingly, Mike claims that more than once he has been warned off investigating the case by anonymous phone calls. Could some vestige of such a cult still be alive?

Another type of sea serpent is known as the marine saurian. It resembles a gigantic crocodile but is far larger than any known species. Some sightings of this monster come from tropical seas where crocodiles are known to live. More problematical are sightings from cooler northern seas.

A marine saurian amazed witnesses at the Shipwright Inn, Pembroke Dock, Wales in March 2004. I visited the pub and spoke with the witnesses.

At 11 a.m. barmaid Lesley John saw something in the waters of the dock: 'It was a big black fin moving slowly through the water drawing ripples after it.' The landlord David Crew and three regular customers ran outside for a closer look. One man, Peter Thomas, was having a meal by the window at the time and said to me:

> 'I saw a diamond shaped, snake-like head lifted up a couple of feet out of the water. It was gliding along smoothly without moving side to side or up and down. It swum against the tide and caused great turbulence. I love the river. I spend most weekends on it; I've never seen anything like this before.'

David Crew added:

> 'It moved smoothly and I felt it had limbs beneath the surface that it propelled itself with. A car ferry goes across that part of the river regularly. The monster was about five times the length of a car.'

A crowed of people had gathered on the dock to watch the monster. A few days later a photo was anonymously dropped into the pub. It shows a huge, crocodile-shaped form in the river. An old sea fort and a promontory of rocks provide a good reference for size. The image matched what the witnesses had seen.

By walking out onto the rocks and looking at the area from both land and water I could gauge the monster's size at 20 metres.

Despite being nine miles inland, Pembroke Dock is the second-deepest natural harbour in the world. Warm currents mean that sea life not usually found in the area abound here, making it a heaven for tourists. Could this have been what attracted the monster?

So what manner of beasts are the reptilian sea serpents? The most popular theory is that they are descendants of prehistoric marine reptiles. In recent years this idea has gone out of fashion in favour of unknown marine mammals. I think that this is very premature. Some sea monsters are undoubtedly marine mammals, but it is my belief that the kinds tackled here are true reptiles.

The plesiosaurs and their gigantic, short-necked relatives the pliosaurs have been touted as favourites in the past. Indeed the long-necked bears a striking resemblance to the plesiosaurs, and the marine saurian is a dead ringer for the crocodile-like pliosaurs. However they belong to a family of reptiles extinct for 65 million years. They died out at the end of the Cretaceous period along with non-avian dinosaurs. But there were other marine reptiles that belong to, or are very closely related to families living today.

The mososaurs were elongate crocodile-like predators with four flippers and savage jaws. Some – such as *Tylosaurus* – grew to twelve metres or more in length. They were not related to the superficially similar-looking pliosaurs, but they were closely related to the varanids or monitor lizards that thrive today.

Another possible sea dragon ancestor was a group of prehistoric marine crocodiles known as Thalattosuchians. Some of these bore fins rather than feet, and some such as *Steneosaurus* and *Metriorychus* were capable of vertical flexation which is a feature reported in the majority of sea serpent cases.

Sixty-five million years of evolution could have adapted such creatures to cope with cold as well as warm water. It could also change their body shape radically, perhaps to compete with the emerging marine mammals.

It seems would-be dragon hunters would do well to seek their quarry in lakes and seas.

Conclusions

Like the hydra the dragon has many faces. One would expect no less from this most ancient of monsters. Most other legendary beasts are restricted in their distribution and influence. The unicorn for example is found in Europe and the Middle East, with an analogue in China. The gryphon is a symbolic beast that was brought to the Greeks via trade routes from Mongolia. It appears in countless statues and paintings but few actually legends refer directly to it. The dragon however is truly universal. There is no doubt that the dragons has been employed as an allegory and has been used as a symbol. Everything from invading armies, floods and solar eclipses have been symbolised by dragons.

The idea of a vast snake may have come from Roman standards. The idea of flight may well also have its genesis in these war like wind socks. Comets and meteors may have added the element of fiery breath to the now airborne serpent.

The screaming hoards of Viking berserkers spilling from their longships may have, with time, being transmuted into stories of ravening dragons. The dragon's love of gold might be a memory of the Danegeld or the plunder the Norse men took. Indeed the idea of a treasure-guarding monster, eternally vigilant, over its hoard of gold seems to have been a Scandinavian concept. Perhaps this is why certain parts of the country, such as the northeast, are richer in dragon lore than others. Simply the influence of the Vikings.

It has been suggested that all dragon lore can be traced back to Greece and the concept of the dragon as a subterranean snake of huge size. Perhaps these were based on pythons brought from India and kept in temples. The dragons that fought Cadamus and Jason were certainly outsized snakes lacking legs or wings. As the Greek / Roman influence spread the giant snake spread with it and took on other attributes as it moved from culture to culture.

It is a neat idea and pleasing to those who seek easy answers. But the dragon as a four footed, two-winged beast is far older. Statues and carvings from Babylon, far older than the Greek or Roman stories, show dragons as we think of them today. They are often shown as casting forth something, possibly fire or venom, from their open jaws. In ancient China too, we see the dragon as a winged quadrupedal reptile. The snake cannot have been the forebear of the dragon. The beast seems to spring almost from nowhere.

There is another intriguing possibility, namely that the dragon was or is still, a real creature. We cannot ignore the wealth of sightings from all over our dragon haunted little planet. The surprising amount of them from modern times argues that there is more here than storyteller's whimsy. There are more sightings every year. By the time this book is published I will have no doubt that I will have heard more.

Dragon lore may be based on glimpses of several species of large reptile currently unknown to science. I have made it my life's work to attempt to find evidence of such creatures and bring them from the darkness of mythology into the light of science.

It would be foolhardy to try to explain such an all-encompassing phenomena with anyone of the explanations above. Indeed it would be doing this most magickal of beasts a disservice to try to pin it down to one thing or one place or one time. The dragon has been with us for thousands of years. It is my belief that it will always be with us. It is interesting to think of what the future holds and what that wonderful word 'dragon' will mean to our descendants.

Works cited

The Book Hunter. Drawing by Ian Brown.

Alderton, David, *Crocodiles and Alligators of the World,* Blandford, 1991.

Alexander, Mark, *The Devil Hunter: The incredible account of the work of a modern day exorcist,* Sphere, 1978.

Appenzella, Tim, Cantley , Donald, and Thomson, David, *Dragons,* Time Life, 1984.

Atkins, William. *The Loch Ness Monster,* Signet, 1977.

Basset, Michale G., *Formed Stones, Folklore and Fossils,* National Museum of Wales, 1984.

Blashford-Snell, Colonel John, *Mysteries,* Bodley Head, 1983.

— *Operation Raleigh,* Collins, 1988.

Bondson, Jan, *The Feejee Mermaid and Other Essays on Natural and Unnatural History,* (Cornell University Press, 1999.

Bord, Janet and Colin, *Alien Animals,* Granada, 1980.

— *Modern Mysteries of Britain,* Grafton Books, 1988.

Broadhurst, Paul and Hamish Miller, *The Sun and the Serpent,* Pendragon Press, 1989.

Bright, Michael, *There are Giants in the Sea,* Robson Books, 1991.

Costello, Peter, *The Magic Zoo,* Sphere, 1979.

Danser, Simon, *The Myths of Reality,* Alternative Albion 2005.

David-Neel, Alexandra, *Magic and Mystery in Tibet,* Crown, 1937.

Dickinson, Peter, *The Flight of Dragons,* Pierrot Publishing, 1979.

Dinsdale, Time, *The Leviathans,* Routledge and Kegan Paul, 1966.

Downes, Jonathan, *The Owlman and Others,* CFZ Publications, 1997.

— *The Rising of The Moon,* Domra, 1999.

Eberhart, George M, *Mysterious Creatures: A guide to cryptozoology,* ABC-CLIO, 2002.

Freeman, Richard, *Dragons: More than a myth?,* CFZ Publications, 2006.

Gilroy, Rex, *Mysterious Australia,* Nexus Publishing, 1995.

Greer, John Michael, *Monsters: An investigation into magical beings,* Llewellyn, 2001.

Griffiths, Bill, *Meet the Dragon: An introduction to Beowulf's adversary,* Heart Of Albion, 1996.

Gould, Charles, *Mythical Monsters,* WH Allen & Co, 1886.

Harrison, Paul, *Sea Serpents and Lake Monsters of the British Isles,* Hale, 2001.

Heuvelmans, Bernard, *On the Track of Unknown Animals,* Rupert Hart-Davis, 1958.

— *In the Wake of the Sea Serpents,* Rupert Hart-Davis, 1968.

Holliday, F.W., *The Dragon and the Disc*, Sidgwick & Jackson, 1973.

— *The Goblin Universe*, Llewellyn, 1986.

Hutton, Ronald, *The Stations of The Sun*, Oxford University Press, 1996.

Ingersoll, Ernest, *Dragons and Dragon Lore*, Payston and Clark, 1928.

Kirk, John, *In the Domain of the Lake Monsters*, Key Porter Books, 1998.

Mackal, Roy, *A Living Dinosaur? In search of Mokele-Mbembe*, E.J. Brill, 1987.

— *Searching for Hidden Animals*, Cadogab Books, 1983.

McBeath, Alistair, *Tiamat's Brood: An Investigation into the Dragons of Ancient Mesopotamia*, Dragon's Head Press, 1999.

McEwan, Graham J., *Mystery Animals of Great Britain and Ireland*, Robert Hayle, 1986.

Michell, John, *The View Over Atlantis*, Sago, 1969.

Needham, Joseph, *Science and Civilisation in China*, Cambridge University Press, 1954.

Newman, Paul, *The Hill of the Dragon*, Kingsmead Press, 1979.

Pennick, Nigel, *Dragons of the West*, Capall Bann, 1997.

Randles, Jenny, *Mind Monsters: Invaders from inner space?*, The Aquarian Press, 1990.

Shiels, Tony, *Monstrum! A wizard's tale*, Fortean Tomes,, 1990.

Shuker, Karl, *Mysteries of Planet Earth*, Carlton, 1999.

— *From Flying Toads to Snakes with Wings*, Llewellyn, 1997.

Simpson, Jacqueline, *British Dragons*, BT Batsford, 1980.

Whitlock, Ralph, *Here be Dragons*, George Allen & Unwin, 1983.

Willoughby-Meade, G., *Chinese Ghouls and Goblins*, Constable, 1928.

Index

Also published by Heart of Albion Press

Mystery Big Cats

Merrily Harpur

In the past twenty years every county in Britain, from Caithness to Cornwall, has had recurrent sightings of 'big cats' – described as being like pumas or panthers. These anomalous big cats sightings are now running at an estimated 1,200 a year.

Farmers, gamekeepers, ornithologists, policemen and even parents on the school run have all been thrilled – or terrified – to see what they assume is a big cat escaped from a zoo. Yet these big cats are neither escapees from zoos nor, as this book conclusively argues, the descendants of pets released into the countryside by their owners in 1976 when the Dangerous Wild Animals Act made it too expensive to keep big cats.

The questions therefore remain, what are they and where have they come from? With the orthodox explanations overturned, Merrily Harpur searches for clues in the cultures of other times and places. She discovers our mystery felines have been with us for longer than we imagine, and throws unexpected light on the way Western civilisation looks at the world.

Mystery Big Cats is the first serious and comprehensive book on the subject. From the drama of eyewitnesses' verbatim accounts to the excitement of new perspectives and insights into a strange and often terrifying experience – it gets to grips with what is now the commonest encounter with the unknown in Britain.

ISBN 1 872883 92 3. Published March 2006. 245 x 175 mm, illustrated, paperback. **£16.95**

A Bestiary of Brass

Peter Heseltine

Peter Heseltine

From antelopes to wyverns, with over fifty species in between, *A Bestiary of Brass* looks the animals, birds, insects, fish – even shellfish – which have been depicted on medieval memorial brasses in Britain. Some are native, others – such as elephants and panthers – were exotic, while dragons and unicorns were as mythical then as they are today.

At the time they were engraved these creatures evoked a wide range of folklore and legends. This rich symbolism is brought to life by the author. But enigmas remain – why would anyone want to be associated with a fox when they were more noted for cunning and slyness, or a hedgehog, or even a whelk? We also find out about the lives of the people commemorated and share the author's detailed knowledge of their heraldic emblems. Practical advice is provided to help make brass rubbings and to learn more about these memorials.

The illustrations show a wide range of the memorials, with detailed views of the creatures they incorporate. *A Bestiary of Brass* will appeal to anyone interested in folklore, art and medieval history. Above all, these masterpieces of craftsmanship reveal that our deep fascination with animals was shared by our ancestors many hundreds of years ago.

EAN 978 1872 883 908. ISBN 1 872883 90 7. March 2006.
Demy 8vo (215 x 138 mm), over 280 illustrations, paperback
£12.95

Also published by Heart of Albion Press

Explore Phantom Black Dogs

edited by Bob Trubshaw

Contributors: Jeremy Harte, Simon
Sherwood, Alby Stone, Bob Trubshaw
and Jennifer Westwood.

The folklore of phantom black dogs is
known throughout the British Isles. From
the Black Shuck of East Anglia to the
Moody Dhoo of the Isle of Man there are
tales of huge spectral hounds 'darker than the night sky' with eyes
'glowing red as burning coals'.

The phantom black dog of British and Irish folklore, which often
forewarns of death, is part of a world-wide belief that dogs are
sensitive to spirits and the approach of death, and keep watch over the
dead and dying. North European and Scandinavian myths dating back
to the Iron Age depict dogs as corpse eaters and the guardians of the
roads to Hell. Medieval folklore includes a variety of 'Devil dogs' and
spectral hounds. Above all, the way people have thought about such
ghostly creatures has steadily evolved.

This book will appeal to all those interested in folklore, the paranormal
and fortean phenomena.

> 'I think this must be the best entry in the Explore series
> I have seen so far... ' **Aeronwy Dafies** *Monomyth
> Supplement*

> 'This is an excellent work and is very highly
> recommended.' **Michael Howard** *The Cauldron*

ISBN 1 872883 78 8. Published 2005. Demy 8vo (215 x 138 mm), 152
+ viii pages, 10 b&w half-tones, paperback. **£12.95**

Also from Heart of Albion Press

Meet the Dragon

An introduction to

Beowulf's adversary

Bill Griffiths

An erudite yet readable insight into the history of dragons, culminating in a detailed discussion of their roles in Old English literature.

'In the natural human order of things, all our attention as readers focuses on those heroes (Beowulf, Sigurðr, St George) whose fortune it is to fight and overcome the repulsive, reptilian foes of mankind we call 'dragons'. The Dragonslayer is a central character in many mythic systems while the fight against the insuperable foe is the crowning glory and bitterest defeat of Beowulf's distinguished career. But what about the dragon? Where does the idea of the dragon come from - given that the creature has no objective reality - and what is its meaning? Why was the business of dragon-slaying the first test that Sigurðr faced, and the final one which Beowulf (and, implicitly, no-one else) could overcome?

'In this neat volume, Bill Griffiths sets out to find answers to the many questions surrounding this richly symbolic creature. In doing so he brings in such matters as human revulsion at the idea of being eaten alive (the fate of animals caught in the coils of the larger serpents) and the relationship between the dragon and the dead - particularly the grave-mound dwelling, treasure-guarding dragons of heroic verse. Bill also discusses the Christian notion of the dragon as one of the beastly manifestations of Satan, and correlates the various concepts underlying the Anglo-Saxon draca to try to bring out the reptile's meaning within the culture (with particular reference to Beowulf, of course).'

Steve Pollington *Wiðowinde*

EAN 978 1872 883 434. ISBN 1 872883 43 5. 1996. A5, 47 pages, illustrated, card covers. **£2.95**

Also from Heart of Albion Press

Explore Fairy Traditions

Jeremy Harte

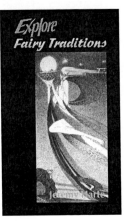

We are not alone. In the shadows of our countryside there lives a fairy race, older than humans, and not necessarily friendly to them. For hundreds of years, men and women have told stories about the strange people, beautiful as starlight, fierce as wolves, and heartless as ice. These are not tales for children. They reveal the fairies as a passionate, proud, brutal people.

Explore Fairy Traditions draws on legends, ballads and testimony from throughout Britain and Ireland to reveal what the fairies were really like. It looks at changelings, brownies, demon lovers, the fairy host, and abduction into the Otherworld. Stories and motifs are followed down the centuries to reveal the changing nature of fairy lore, as it was told to famous figures like W.B. Yeats and Sir Walter Scott. All the research is based on primary sources and many errors about fairy tradition are laid to rest.

Jeremy Harte combines folklore scholarship with a lively style to show what the presence of fairies meant to people's lives. Like their human counterparts, the secret people could kill as well as heal. They knew marriage, seduction, rape and divorce; they adored some children and rejected others. If we are frightened of the fairies, it may be because their world offers an uncomfortable mirror of our own.

'*Explore Fairy Traditions* **is an excellent introduction to the folklore of fairies, and I would highly recommend it.**' Paul Mason *Silver Wheel*

ISBN 1 872883 61 3. **Published 2004.**
Demi 8vo (215 x 138 mm), 171 + vi pages, 6 line drawings, paperback. **£9.95**

Explore Folklore

Bob Trubshaw

**'A howling success, which plugs
a big and obvious gap'**

Professor Ronald Hutton

There have been fascinating developments in the study of folklore in the last twenty-or-so years, but few books about British folklore and folk customs reflect these exciting new approaches. As a result there is a huge gap between scholarly approaches to folklore studies and 'popular beliefs' about the character and history of British folklore. *Explore Folklore* is the first book to bridge that gap, and to show how much 'folklore' there is in modern day Britain.

Explore Folklore shows there is much more to folklore than morris dancing and fifty-something folksingers! The rituals of 'what we do on our holidays', funerals, stag nights and 'lingerie parties' are all full of 'unselfconscious' folk customs. Indeed, folklore is something that is integral to all our lives – it is so intrinsic we do not think of it as being 'folklore'.

The implicit ideas underlying folk lore and customs are also explored. There might appear to be little in common between people who touch wood for luck (a 'tradition' invented in the last 200 years) and legends about people who believe they have been abducted and subjected to intimate body examinations by aliens. Yet, in their varying ways, these and other 'folk beliefs' reflect the wide spectrum of belief and disbelief in what is easily dismissed as 'superstition'.

Explore Folklore provides a lively introduction to the study of most genres of British folklore, presenting the more contentious and profound ideas in a readily accessible manner.

ISBN 1 872883 60 5. Published 2002.
Perfect bound, demi 8vo (215x138 mm), 200 pages, **£9.95**

Explore Mythology

Bob Trubshaw

Myths are usually thought of as something to do with 'traditional cultures'. The study of such 'traditional' myths emphasises their importance in religion, national identity, hero-figures, understanding the origin of the universe, and predictions of an apocalyptic demise. The academic study of myths has done much to fit these ideas into the preconceived ideas of the relevant academics.

Only in recent years have such long-standing assumptions about myths begun to be questioned, opening up whole new ways of thinking about the way such myths define and structure how a society thinks about itself and the 'real world'.

These new approaches to the study of myth reveal that, to an astonishing extent, modern day thinking is every bit as 'mythological' as the world-views of, say, the Classical Greeks or obscure Polynesian tribes. Politics, religions, science, advertising and the mass media are all deeply implicated in the creation and use of myths.

Explore Mythology provides a lively introduction to the way myths have been studied, together with discussion of some of the most important 'mythic motifs' – such as heroes, national identity, and 'central places' – followed by a discussion of how these ideas permeate modern society. These sometimes contentious and profound ideas are presented in an easily readable style of writing.

ISBN 1 872883 62 1. Published 2003.
Perfect bound. Demi 8vo (215 x 138 mm), 220 + xx pages, 17 line drawings. **£9.95**

The Enchanted Land

Myths and Legends of Britain's Landscape

Revised, fully illustrated edition

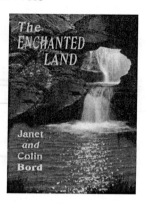

Janet and Colin Bord

Britain's landscape is overlain by a magic carpet of folklore and folktales, myths and legends. Enchantment and legend still lurk in places as diverse as hills and mountains, rivers and streams, caves and hollows, springs and wells, cliffs and coasts, pools and lakes, and rocks and stones.

The dramatic stories woven around these places tell of sleeping knights, beheaded saints, giants, dragons and monsters, ghosts, King Arthur, mermaids, witches, hidden treasure, drowned towns, giant missiles, mysterious footprints, visits to Fairyland, underground passages, human sacrifices, and much more.

The 'Places to Visit' section locates and describes in detail more than 50 sites.

This revised edition is fully illustrated, with around 130 photographs and illustrations.

Janet and Colin Bord live in North Wales, where they run the Fortean Picture Library. They have written more than 20 books since their first successful joint venture, *Mysterious Britain* in 1972.

From reviews of the first edition:

'Janet's own enthusiasm for a number of the sites is conveyed vividly and lends credibility to the notion that Britain is still an enchanted land.' *Mercian Mysteries*

ISBN 1 872883 91 5. March 2006. 245 x 175 mm, over 200 illustrations, paperback **£16.95**

Heart of Albion

The UK's leading publisher of
folklore, mythology and cultural studies.

Further details of all Heart of Albion titles online at
www.hoap.co.uk

All titles available direct from Heart of Albion Press.
Please add £1.30 p&p (UK only; email
albion@indigogroup.co.uk for overseas postage).

To order books or request our current catalogue please contact

Heart of Albion Press
2 Cross Hill Close, Wymeswold
Loughborough, LE12 6UJ

Phone: 01509 880725
Fax: 01509 881715
email: albion@indigogroup.co.uk
Web site: www.hoap.co.uk